SRI SWAMI CHIDANANDAJI

GOD AS MOTHER

SWAMI CHIDANANDA

Published By

THE DIVINE LIFE SOCIETY
P.O. SHIVANANDANAGAR—249 192
Distt. Tehri-Garhwal, U.P., Himalayas, India

Price]   1991   [Rs. 15/=

Fourth Edition : 1991
(3000 Copies)

Printed in sacred memory of
LATE MRS. RATNABAI KRISHNARAO BELLARE
(1000 Copies)

ISBN 81-7052-090-8

Published by Swami Krishnananda for the Divine Life
Society, Shivanandanagar, and printed by him at the
Yoga-Vedanta Forest Academy Press, P.O. Shivanandanagar,
Distt. Tehri-Garhwal, U.P., Himalayas, India

LATE MRS. RATNABAI
KRISHNARAO BELLARE

To
The Supreme Mother
This Flower
Is offered in humility and reverence

To

The Supreme Mother

This Flower

Is offered in humility and reverence

PUBLISHERS' NOTE

During the Navaratra Durga Puja at the Sivananda Ashram, Rishikesh, in 1953 (8th to 17th October), Revered Sri Swami Chidanandaji Maharaj delivered a series of most illuminating lectures on "God as Mother" which have been brought together in a book form.

These lectures contain in them an inspiring message to all sections and strata of mankind. That it has already gone through three editions before this, gives ample credence that it was well received by readers. Besides being out of print for quite some time, we felt it most fitting to bring out this fourth edition under the auspices of the Amrita Mahotsava of Pujya Sri Swami Chidanandaji Maharaj.

24.9.1991   —THE DIVINE LIFE SOCIETY

PRAYER TO MOTHER

Salutations to the Divine Mother who exists in all beings in the form of intelligence, mercy and beauty, salutations, O Sweet Mother, the consort of Lord Siva. O Mother Parvati! Thou art Lakshmi, Thou art Sarasvati. Thou art Kali, Durga and Kundalini Shakti. Thou art in the form of all objects. Thou art the sole refuge of all. Thou hast enchanted the whole world. The whole universe is the play of Thy three Gunas. How can I praise Thee? Thy glory is indescribable. Thy splendour is ineffable. Protect me. Guide me, O Loving Mother!

O Adorable Mother! Thou hast generated this great illusion by which all people walk deluded in this world. All sciences have come from Thee. Without Thy grace, no one can get success in spiritual Sadhana and salvation in the end. Thou art the seed for this world. Thou hast two aspects, viz., the unmanifested aspect or Avyaktam and the manifested aspect or the gross universe. The whole world gets dissolved in Avyaktam during Pralaya. Give me the divine eye. Let me behold Thy real majestic form. Help me to cross over this illusion, O Kind Mother!

O Compassionate Mother! I bow to Thee. Thou art my saviour. Thou art my goal. Thou art my sole support. Thou art my guide and the remover of all afflictions, troubles and miseries. Thou art the embodiment of auspiciousness. Thou pervadest the whole universe. The whole universe is filled with Thee. Thou art the store-house of all qualities. Do Thou protect me. I again and again salute Thee. O Glorious Mother! Salutations to Thee. All women are Thy parts. Mind, egoism, intellect, body, Prana, senses, are Thy forms. Thou art Para Shakti and Apara Prakriti. Thou art electricity, magnetism, force, energy, power and will. All forms are Thy forms only. Reveal to me the mystery of creation. Bestow on me the divine knowledge.

O Loving Mother! Thou art the primal energy. Thou hast two aspects, namely, the terrible and peaceful. Thou art modesty, gentleness, shyness, generosity, courage, forbearance and patience. Thou art faith in the heart of devotees and generosity in noble people, chivalry in warriors and ferocity in tigers. Give me strength to control the mind and the Indriyas. Make me worthy to dwell in Thee. Salutations unto Thee.

O Mother Supreme! When shall I have equal vision and placid state of mind? When shall I be established in Ahimsa, Satyam and Brahmacharya? When shall I have Thy cosmic vision? When shall I get deep abiding peace and perennial joy? When shall I enter into deep meditation and Samadhi?

O Radiant Mother! I have not done any spiritual Sadhana or service of teachers. I have not practised any Vrata, pilgrimage, charity, Japa and meditation or worship. I have not studied religious scriptures. I have neither discrimination nor dispassion. I have neither purity nor burning desire for liberation. Thou art my sole refuge. Thou art my only support. My silent adorations unto Thee. I am Thy meek suppliant. Remove the veil of ignorance.

O Gracious Mother! Prostrations unto Thee. Where art Thou? Do not forsake me. I am Thy child. Take me to the other shore of fearlessness and joy. When shall I behold Thy lotus feet with my own eyes? Thou art the boundless ocean of mercy. When philosopher's stone turns iron into gold by contact, when the Ganges turns impure water into pure water, can'st Thou not turn me, O Divine Mother, into a pure soul? May my tongue repeat Thy Name always!

(*Sri Swami Sivananda* in GEMS OF PRAYERS)

THE INDIAN CONCEPT OF THE DIVINE MOTHER

(Sri Swami Sivananda)

Since the dawn of civilisation, when the primitive man lived in a matriarchal society, the worship of the Divine Mother came into practice. Later on, as civilisation progressed, the matriarchal pattern gradually faded out, and the father became the head of the family unit, where he was treated as the man in authority and to whom everyone looked for guidance and approval. Consequently, there was a change in the concept of God as such; the Fatherhood of God was established. But Mother worship persisted simultaneously, since this concept was psychologically more appealing to the devotee, the mother being nearest in filial affection to the child. Subsequently, a synthetic harmony between the Motherhood and Fatherhood of God was developed by the Hindu religion; the people worshipped Sita and Rama, or Radha and Krishna together.

The concept of the human mind is based on relative experience. Subjective idealism, therefore, in its initial stages, takes the aid of objective and relative analogies. God is neither limited to abstract or concrete concepts. But it is easier to establish a conscious relationship with the Providence in terms of benevolent fatherhood or affectionate, kindly motherhood than by the concept of an unfathomable void. God is devoid of qualities, in reality, but a relative superimposition of the positive ideals of goodness and virtue is essential for self-culture and spiritual progress of the aspirant.

Mother is very kind to her child. You are more free with your mother than with anybody else. It is the mother who protects you, nourishes you, consoles you, cheers you and nurses you. She is your first preceptor. She sacrifices her all for the sake of her children. In the spiritual field also, the aspirant has very intimate relationship with the Divine Mother.

The Upasana or the worship of the Universal Mother leads to the attainment of knowledge of the Self. The Yaksha Prasna in Kenopanishad supports this view. Approach Her with an open heart. Lay bare your mind with frankness and humility. Lay your thoughts be pure and sublime. Become as simple as a child. Pulverise your individual entity, the egoistic nature, cunningness, selfishness and crookedness. Make a total, unreserved, ungrudging self-surrender to Her. Chant Her Mantras. Worship Her with faith and devotion.

Navaratri is the most suitable occasion for doing intense Sadhana. These nine days are very sacred to Mother. Plunge yourself in Her worship. It is an occasion symbolising the victory of the higher, divine forces over the lower, negative qualities that find their expression in injustice, oppression, aggrandisement, greed, selfishness, hatred and a host of other undivine forces that add to the suffering of man.

Worship the Mother in all Her manifestations. She is the creative aspect of the Absolute. She is symbolised as Cosmic Energy. Energy is the physical ultimate of all forms of matter and the sustaining force of the Spirit. Energy and Spirit are inseparable. They are essentially one. The five elements and their combinations are the external manifestations of the Mother. Intelligence, discrimination, psychic power and will are Her internal manifestations. Humanity is Her visible form. Service of humanity is, therefore, the worship of the Divine Mother.

Feel that the Mother sees through your eyes, hears through your ears, and works through your hands. Feel that the body, mind, Prana, intellect and all their functions are Her manifestations. The one, universal life throbs in the heart of all. How can there be any room for hatred and selfishness, when by hating another you are but hating the Mother, when by being selfish to another you are but denying your own self. Drive deep this consciousness within your heart. Always meditate and practise this ideal of divine oneness.

Mother's grace is boundless. Her mercy is illimitable. She is pleased with a little purity of heart. The sacred Navaratri is approaching. Do not lose this glorious opportunity. Make a definite and sincere attempt to obtain the grace of the Mother. She will transform your entire life, and bless you with the milk of divine wisdom, spiritual insight and Kaivalya!

May you all obtain the grace of Mother Durga!

THE WORSHIP OF THE DIVINE MOTHER

(*Sri Swami Sivananda*)

Devi is synonymous with Shakti or the Divine Power that manifests, sustains and transforms the universe as the one unifying Force of Existence. In fact, worship of Devi is not sectarian, it does not belong to any cult. By Drive or Shakti we mean the presupposition of all forms of existential power, the power of knowledge, of omniscience. These powers are the glorious attributes of God—you may call Him Vishnu or Siva or as you like. In other words, Shakti is the very possibility of the Absolute's appearing as many, of God's causing this universe. Shakti and Shakta are one; the power and the one who possesses the power cannot be separated; God and Shakti are like fire and heat of fire.

Devi-worship or Shakti-worship is therefore worship of God's glory, of God's greatness and supremacy. It is adoration of the Almighty. It is unfortunate that Devi is misunderstood as a bloodthirsty 'Hindu Goddess.' No. Devi is not the property of the Hindu alone. Devi does not belong to any religion. Devi is the conscious power of the Deva. Let this never be forgotten. The words Devi, Shakti, etc. and the ideas of the different forms connected with these names are concessions given to the limitations of human knowledge; human comprehension. Bhagavan Sri Krishna says in the Gita, "This is only my lower nature Shakti, beyond this is my higher nature, the Original Shakti, the life principle which sustains this entire universe." The Upanishad says, "The Para Shakti, the Supreme Power of this God is heard of in various ways, this power is the nature of God manifesting as knowledge, strength and activity." Truly speaking all beings of the universe are Shakti worshippers, for there is none who does not love and long for power in some form or other. Physicists and scientists have proved now that everything is pure imperishable energy. This energy is only a form of Divine Shakti which exists on every form of existence.

Since Shakti cannot be worshipped in its essential nature, it is worshipped as conceived of in its manifestations, viz., creation, preservation and destruction. Shakti in relation to these three functions is Sarasvati, Lakshmi and Kali. These, as is evident, are not three distinct Devis, but the one formless Devi worshipped in three different forms. Navaratri is the festive occasion of the 'nine-day-worship of Maha-Kali, Maha-Lakshmi and Maha-Sarasvati' the Divinity of the Universe adored in three ways.

Sarasvati is cosmic Intelligence, cosmic consciousness, cosmic knowledge. Worship of Sarasvati is necessary for Buddhi-Shuddi, Viveka-Udaya, Vichara-Shakti for Jnana for Self-illumination. Lakshmi does not mean mere material wealth like gold, cattle, etc. All kinds of prosperity, glory, magnificence, joy, exaltation or greatness come under the grace of Goddess Lakshmi. Sri Appayya Dikshitar calls even final Liberation as "Moksha Samrajya Lakshmi." Hence worship of Lakshmi means the worship of Divinity, the power that dissolves multiplicity in unity. The worship of Devi is therefore the explanation of the entire process of spiritual Sadhana in all its aspect.

During Navaratri, observe strict *anushthana*, and purify your inner spiritual nature. This is the most auspicious time in the year for Mother-Worship. Read Sapthasathi, or Devi Mahatmya and Lalita Sahasranama. Do Japa of the Mantra of Devi. Perform formal worship with purity and sincerity and absolute devotion. Cry for the Darshan of Mother Devi. The Divine Mother will bless you with the knowledge, the peace and the joy that know no end. May the Divine Mother bless you all!

CONTENTS

ॐ ह्रीं ॐ

GOD AS MOTHER

ऐं ह्रीं क्लीं चामुण्डायै विच्चे

FIRST NIGHT

THE POWER OF THE TRANSCENDENT REALITY

या देवी सर्वभूतेषु विष्णुमायेति शब्दिता ।
नमस्तस्यै नमस्तस्यै नमस्तस्यै नमो नमः ॥

PROSTRATIONS again and again to the blessed Divine Mother who is the source, substratum and the ultimate goal of all creation.

The Mother is a mysterious, indescribable power of the Supreme Being. She is the dynamic aspect of the Supreme, Transcendent Being, which is infinity, eternity and ineffable peace, beyond the cognisance of the senses and the mind.

Upon this very solemn and holy occasion which marks the commencement of the sacred annual nine-day worship of the Deity in Its aspect as the Supreme Mother, the first day of the Navaratra culminating in Vijayadasami, popularly known as the Dussera, it is a great mark of divine grace and blessing that we have the privilege of gathering together and glorifying the Mother, speaking a few words about the Divine Mother, adoring Her and worshipping Her and praying for Her Grace, the Grace which alone can enable us to attain success and fruition in all endeavours be they material or spiritual, secular or sacred; by which alone a seeker is able to reach the end of his quest and the Sadhaka is able to achieve the Thing for which he strives, the soul is able to attain perfection and to realise the Infinite. The Grace of the Mother is an indispensable factor to attain Moksha-Siddhi. Upon this sacred occasion, let us try to know a few things about the Indian conception of the Divine Mother and about the significance as well as the traditional background of this nine-day worship.

In India the Hindus fall under four or five broad religious divisions. There are the worshippers of the Supreme Being in its aspect as Siva; we call them the Saivites. Then there are the worshippers of the selfsame Supreme Being in its aspect as Vishnu. Them we call Vaishnavas. There is still a third section of people—and quite a number of them—who worship the one God, the Supreme Being, but as manifest in the form of the great Goddess, the Devi Shakti. They are referred to as Shaktas. There again are two lessknown sects called the Ganapatyas who worship the Supreme Being as Ganapaty, and the Souryas or the worshippers of the Supreme Being manifest as the splendrous light as embodied in the visible orb of the sun, the giver of light, the sustainer of the life-process in this world of ours.

The Navaratra worship of the Devi is eminently a Shakta-worship, and it has come down to us through the Shakta-tradition. A very great section of these

Shaktas are localised in the Province of Bengal and Assam. Their supreme scripture, glorifying the Divine mother, is known as the Durga Saptashati or the Devi Mahatmya. It is known by the name Saptashati because it is a book of 700 verses. In Bengali it is familiarly known as the Chandi; also in these parts—Garhwal—people refer to the reading of the Devi Mahatmya as *Chandi-Patha*. This is derived from one of the names of the Divine Mother Herself who is called Chandika.

The reading of the scripture is done in a very scientific manner. There is a strict procedure laid down by the Shastras. In the first part which was read today there is a detailed exposition of the Devi Tattva. The setting is in the form of a story; and the exposition is given by a sage to a king and a merchant. It is full of deep philosophic truth in regard to the aspect of the Deity, Her nature, how She is and what She is. There are sublime, elevating hymns glorifying the Mother; and the ways of propitiating Her are given. The very reading of the scripture from start to finish is itself a very great and effective Sadhana in the Shakta mode of worship and spiritual practice. I shall just give in a few words the essence of the scripture.

Essence of Devi Mahatmya

It begins this way. A king of the Surya Vamsa to which Lord Rama also belonged, named Suratha, is overcome and overwhelmed by his foes, who compel him to flee his kingdom. He takes shelter in a forest. He is deeply afflicted and dejected, deprived of all his wealth and retinue; and he is wandering forlorn, destitute of everything, in a very wretched condition. His mind again and again goes back to the bitter fate which he has suffered. Thinks of his kingdom, his wealth, his ministers and the way in which the kingdom is likely to be governed under the new rulers. While he is in this state of mind, he happens to come to the vicinity of the hermitage of a great God-realised sage, called Rishi Medha. He sees the hermitage with all its beauty, the disciples of the Rishi—everything pervaded by serenity, calmness and purity; and he stays there.

While he is in this hermitage he comes across a fellow-sufferer, a brother-in-distress, a man named Samadhi, belonging to the merchant community, who has also similarly run away from his home because of misfortune. He had lost all his wealth to his own relatives; and his own family had turned him out of the house. He is thus forced to wander into the forest. He also takes shelter at the feet of the sage.

They find that they are more or less in the same predicament, deprived of their wealth and ousted from their home, with their own people turned against them; and in spite of all this unkindness of their own people, both of them are intrigued and deeply puzzled to find that with all the hostility and enmity of their people, yet their minds go again and again back to these very people, to the very things which have been the cause of their sorrow, of their grief, of their deep disappointment and dejection.

They try to discuss this between themselves; what is this mysterious nature of the mind which harkens back again and again and clings to those self-same things and people from whom they have had nothing but pain and sorrow. Unable to solve this riddle, they go and humbly entreat the Rishi Medha to throw some light upon this problem. They, ask the Rishi: "O Wise One, pray throw some light upon this problem; we are greatly puzzled to find this mind still clings to those very objects, is attached to those very persons, from whom it has received the greatest pain and sorrow; it knows there is no pleasure in those things, yet it will not give up its attachment to them—what is the reason for this, how do you explain this peculiar delusion of the mind?"

In answer to this query which, though it has been put into the mouth of Raja Suratha and Vaishya Samadhi, yet is a universal question which agitates the minds of all thinking men and women all over the world, Rishi Medha gives his wondrous exposition of the greatness of the Devi. He says; "O my children! A mysterious delusion dwells in the mind of man, by which his pure reason is blinded, by which delusion he is again and again made to cling and go back to those very objects and persons from which he is subject to so much pain and suffering. This delusion, this veiling power, is really the mysterious power of the divine Mother. It is She who is the cosmic illusion. It is She who is at the back of projection of this very universe itself. It is with Her mysterious veiling Power that the one seems to have become the many, the formless

seems to have taken numerous forms and the unmanifest seems to have become manifest and this
mysterious power is the indescribable power of the
Supreme Being itself. It is Brahma Shakti; it is the
Mahamaya or the great Cosmic Illusory Power which
emanates from the Lord Himself, and it is through this
power that the Lord sets going this universal drama of
projection of creation, preservation and once again the
ultimate dissolution of all names and forms back into
its pristine transcendental state of Pure Being."

The King Suratha and Vaishya Samadhi want to
know more about the mysterious power which Rishi
Medha has referred to and to know more about this
cosmic power which is at the back of all manifestation. In response to this request of theirs Rishi Medha
goes into the detailed exposition of the nature of the
divine Mother; and the 700-versed scripture contains
this exposition. In the end, having expounded the
mystery and secret of the supreme nature of the divine
Mother Rishi Medha advises Suratha and Samadhi to
go and practise Yoga, worship the Divine Mother, pray
to Her and meditate upon Her and propitiate Her.
Thus propitiated She becomes manifest to them and
bestows Her Grace upon both the king and the merchant and their heart's desire is fulfilled.

This in short is the import of this supreme scripture of the Shaktas—Devi Mahatmya.

Maya and Brahman Are One

This exposition of the Devi Tattva goes to explain
to us how the Supreme Shakti is all in all. It tells us

that whatever we see, whatever we perceive in this phenomenal universe before us, is nothing but the outcome of this supreme power of the Para Brahman, viz. the primal force. She is called the Adi-Shakti. She is also known as the transcendental power—Para-Shakti. She is known as the superlative, the great power—Maha-Shakti.

What exactly is the relationship between this great Divine Power and the ultimate Supreme Being the Almighty, is a question that is very interesting and which occupies the minds of all great thinkers. Varied explanations have been given but sages of realisation have stated in illuminating terms the secret of this relationship between the deity as they conceived of in its aspect of Supreme Mother and the deity in its transcendental aspect. We are told how the Para Brahman and His Supreme Mysterious Power of World-illusion whom we call Maya or Devi are in fact one and the same in essence. They are apparently different, but yet they are one. It is a distinction without a difference in fact. That is the relationship between them. As it were they are the obverse and the reverse of the self-same coin. You cannot conceive of the Para Brahman without conceiving of the Devi; and the conception of the Devi automatically pre-supposes the conception of the Para-Brahman. They explain to us how the Devi or the Supreme Divine Mother is the mysterious link between the manifest and the unmanifest. She is the medium that connects the unmanifest with the manifest. For instance, there is an effect and a cause which is responsible for this ef-

fect—but what is the thing which connects the effect
with the cause and the cause with the effect? There
is some mysterious link which connects these two and
makes them one. Though apparently two, they are in
reality two terminals of the self-same process. This
process of the cause becoming manifest as the effect,
this power that makes the cause appear as the effect
is known as the Maya, the illusion or the Devi.

The Supreme Brahman is also described as per-
fectly beyond all movement and motion because being
of the nature of limitlessness and infinity the very
question of motion does not arise. The Supreme
Power whom we call Devi is described as the dynamic
aspect of the Para Brahman. They say that they are
as inseparable as the whiteness of the milk and the
milk; as the heat and fire; as a snake and its zigzag
motion. The moment you think of milk, automatically
you think of whiteness. The moment you think of fire,
you posit also the heat. If the burning property is
taken away from fire, you can no longer call it fire.
Even so, Para Brahman and Shakti are as inseparable
as the burning property of fire and fire itself. If Brahman is fire, Shakti or Devi is the burning property of
fire. A more up-to-date analogy which we can draw to
illustrate the mysterious connection between Maya or
Prakriti or Shakti and Brahman is this. We have the
power of electricity when it is inside a battery. When
the power of electricity is here within the battery, it
is not manifest. It is not dynamic. It is static. The battery can be taken from place to place: no one will
know that it holds within itself the tremendous force.

There is no indication to give us an idea that it contains within itself this marvellous power. But the moment this self-same electric current is made to spring into dynamism through a system of wiring through a circuit, we find this static force springs into a wonderful dynamism. It travels with lightning speed; it is able to give a shock; or to make an electric bulb spring into incandescence and manifest as light; it manifests itself as the whirling motion in a fan; it manifests itself as freezing cold within the refrigerator and as abnormal power of heat in an electric heater; it is able to burn things; it manifests as sound in an electric siren—this power which is held in a static form within a battery becomes manifest as light, motion, heat, cold, sound and any number of aspects manifest and tangible and perceivable through the senses. Even so the Supreme Power in its transcendental motionless static aspect known as the Para Brahman is nameless, formless, unmanifest and the self-same supreme power when it springs into manifestation, into creativity, is projected as names and forms, into countless dynamic forces which pervade the entire phenomenal world. Mother is electricity, the brightness of the sun, the depth of the ocean, movement in the hand, the smell and fragrance in flowers, the musical note in sound, everything in this universe, invisible as well as visible, all motion, all force, all movements; and She is present in the human being as intelligence, as mind, as Vrittis, as emotions—everything that we perceive in this world either within the individual or without in the forces of nature. She is the very life of the universe. She is the very source, the sustainer and ultimate dissolver of the universe. *Sarvam Shaktimayam Jagat*; this is the ultimate truth. Whatever there is in the universe from the grossest thing to the subtlest, the least to the greatest—everything is the variegated manifestation of the Supreme Mother Herself, the Transcendental Power of the Supreme Being. It is this cosmic Power who appears as all names and forms, who is the very source of all embodiment, of all manifestation. It is on account of the Mother that manifestation is made possible.

It is this Supreme Force that we worship during the nine days through the medium of certain forms. This great power of all powers is conceived of by the devout worshipper in certain distinct aspects—in her three aspects as Mahakali or Durga, Mahalakshmi and as Mahasaraswati. The nine-day worship is divided into three groups of three days each—the first three days we worship the Mother as manifest in and through the form of Mahakali or Durga. During the second group of three days we worship the Divine Mother as manifest in and through our conception of the form of Mahalakshmi. And during the last three days we worship Her in and through the form of Mahasaraswati. This particular order of the worship has got a very deep and very vital meaning, about which we shall refer during the subsequent days.

SECOND NIGHT

THE DESTROYER OF DESTRUCTIVE FORCES

या देवी सर्वभूतेषु शक्तिरूपेण संस्थिता ।
नमस्तस्यै नमस्तस्यै नमस्तस्यै नमो नमः ॥

SALUTATIONS again and again to the blessed divine mother, the Supreme Inscrutable Power, the mysterious Achintya Shakti of para Brahman. Salutations to the great Devi who is the source of all manifestation and embodiment. Salutations to the great Divine Power, Divya Shakti, from whom have flowed forth all the countless, innumerable universes, in whom all manifestations have their being and into whom all names and forms dissolve and vanish, and through whom all beings attain their eternal union with the great reality, the Supreme Transcendental Being, Para Brahman.

This conception of the great power, the Cosmic Spirit, as the Mother is very easy to understand. For the first impression of any soul who has come out into this world is that of the mother. The earliest recollection which a being can ever have is that of lying in his or her mother's lap and perhaps looking up and gazing into the love-filled eyes of the mother. To the child in the mother is centered a whole world of tenderness, of love, of nourishment and of care. It is the ideal world from where one draws sustenance, where one runs for comfort, which one clings to for protection and nourishment; and there he gets comfort, protection and care. Therefore, the ideal of love, care and protection is in the conception of the mother. Therefore, this notion transferred to the Cosmic Being is the most natural, most logical and most easy-to-be understood step, and thus it is that the glorified conception of the great mother who loves all, nourishes all, cares for all and protects all, has come into being in the philosophic conception of the Hindu.

Today we shall devoutly offer our humble worship at the Mother's Blessed Feet in the form of a few words describing some aspects of Her glory. In doing this, let us ever be aware that even this privilege of worshipping Her; glorifying Her and dwelling upon Her greatness is only due to Her compassion and Grace. Without Her Grace, most difficult it is to get an opportunity to think of Her, to remember Her, and to speak of Her, and to utter Her glorious names, calling upon Her as Mother. All-gracious is She, infinitely compassionate is She; love is her Nature and thus She has bestowed upon us all this great blessing and the joy to dwell upon Her in thought and through word to devoutly adore Her upon this most auspicious and glorious day.

The Mother is whatever is. The essence of pure existence is the Supreme Being or Para Brahman. Mother is whatever is that we know. That which is beyond our knowledge, that is the Purusha, the Supreme Being, the transcendental Para Brahman. That which we know through our mind and senses is nothing but the manifestation of Mother. She is not only the Universe which we know, this little world and the countless stars, the sun and moon—all these the terrestrial and the stellar, the lunar and the solar systems that comprise this little universe; all this is but an infinitesimal speck in the vastness and infinity that Mother is. Innumerable such universes have their rise and fall within Her infinite nature. She is all-power and also the great transcendental power at the back of all manifestation, the primal cause for all manifestation and embodiment. She is the very creatrix not only of this world but even the creator, preserver and dissolver of the world. Brahma, Vishnu and Maheshwara have their being in the Mother. She is the Mother of all, countless Brahmas, Vishnus and Maheshwaras. In as much as She is all-power, all powers are Her play; and therefore all the three dynamic manifestations Brahma, Vishnu and Maheshwara also are modifications of Mother as Adi-Shakti. She is also Brahma-Shakti manifest to us in and through the form of Saraswati, Vishnu-Shakti manifest in and through the form of Lakshmi, and also Siva-Shakti manifest in and through the form of Parvati.

Delusion and Deliverance

In this aspect of all power, She has a twofold form. The devout Hindu worships Her as both. It is a beautiful conception: and what a wonderful depth of significance there is in this conception of Mother in Her twofold aspects—that of the Cosmic Delusion as well as of the Cosmic Deliverance! She binds down all to this mysterious illusory appearance, this world-play, and turns them in her own playful manner in the wheel of birth and death. As such She is known by the name Avidya, the delusion that is opposed to spiritual wisdom or knowledge. She is also the Cosmic Deliverance. In this aspect She smiles upon Her children and She releases them from the delusion of Her other aspect Avidya. In Her aspect as this Cosmic Deliverance, we know of the Mother as Vidya-Maya. Artists have therefore visualised Her in the form of a radiant being, a Goddess, having in one hand a noose or a type of rope by which She binds, and in the other hand a sharp knife by which She snaps the bondage if She is propitiated. Thus she is a mysterious combination of Avidya Maya and Vidya Maya. Therefore, She is called Indescribable.

In both these aspects She has set up the Drama of universal phenomena. Lovers of the Mother who have worshipped Her and obtained Her Grace and have been vouchsafed with a vision of Her real nature have lovingly depicted Mother and Her play in this secret way. We all know that as children when in a group we gather together, we wish to play; and not knowing how we may carry on this play we approach the grandmother of the house. Lovingly she consents to show us a game; and thus she sets going a game of hide-and-seek. She tells the children: Children, run about and play. The children engage themselves in play. They run; they catch each other and the game of hide-and-seek goes on. But, then, should some child feel that it has had enough of the play and wish that it may be released from the play, tired of running here and there it has only to run up to the grand dame and lay its hand upon her. One who touches the grand dame cannot now be caught. Even as the grand dame brought about this play, watches the play in progress, and takes care of the children at play, and in the end touching her the child is released from the play,—even so, this universe is but a child's play to the great Mother. Anyone who is fed up with this constant running about in this wilderness of the sense-world and longs to be out of the play, he has but to run up to this great Mother and touch Her; and once for all he is released from the bondage of this play. Thus have devotees of the Mother sweetly and intimately conceived of this world-play with the Mother as both; one who initiates it and one who ends it.

The Puzzling Kali

When we step into the further consideration of particular aspects of the Devi immediately we are confronted by a terrible problem. For the very first conception of the Mother, especially as it is done during the Devi Puja is in a form and in an aspect which leaves ordinary minds quite bewildered—not only those who are foreign to our culture and genius but even Indians, even Hindus, many of them enlightened and educated, are unable to understand what is this conception of divinity whom we call mother as an all-destructive terrible, and fearful being?

In Bengal, the whole of the Dussera worship is the worship of Durga and Mahakali. To very many people Kali is a name that strikes terror. We Hindus even think that Kali-worshippers are Tamasic and that Kali is a dread deity. I can say from my own personal experience that if a picture of Mahakali with Her dark body, lolling red tongue, with Her garland of skulls, dressed in a skirt made of severed human hands, with a sword dripping blood in Her hand—if such a picture is kept in an orthodox South Indian house, the ladies of the house will see that the picture is forthwith removed from the house. If their feelings about the divinity as Kali was right, then how comes this conception of Kali as the mother? How can you worship Her?

It is a natural mistake which requires to be corrected. Mother is never terrible, never fearful, is always all-loving and all-compassionate. The explanation for the divine Mother Parashakti being conceived of, among other aspects, also in Her aspect as Kali is a very simple one. It is not difficult; it is not deeply metaphysical; it is not obscurely philosophical; it is very natural and very simple.

I shall first start by giving a very up-to-date and modern, and therefore, easily graspable analogy. We have the modern antibiotics the various *mycins* and also Penicillin. They are called the life-savers of the modern age and millions of people look upon them with feelings of gratitude. But though these life-saving drugs which are benign and cure disease, are the benefactors of humanity, I shall show how they may be also regarded to be terrible and destructive. They are destructive to the germs which they attack in the system and destroy. You get infected; your body is filled with germs; they cause disease. You take penicillin and it goes and destroys all the germs; and by thus annihilating and destroying these germs, the disease is removed and you become well. Would it be correct to call these life-saving antibiotics very destructive? If it were right to call them destructive and terrible, then you may also be equally right to call Kali the mother, terrible and destructive.

Destroys to Save

For, She destroys but to save. She destroys ignorance, nescience, in order to bestow knowledge. She destroys darkness so that we may realise light. She destroys all pain, all sorrow, all misery and all the earthly travails and tribulations; and bestows upon us bliss, joy and immortality. Thus She is a destroyer of all those factors that bind the Jiva to this terrible Samsara. She is a terrible destroyer of all terrible things and the benign bestower of blessedness and beatitude. Thus it is that the Mother is conceived of as the destroyer of one of Her own aspects; just as by the power of will—and will is also a portion of the mind—we overcome certain weaknesses and evils in the same mind. As Vidya-Maya, Mother using Her aspect as

Kali, destroys Avidya and takes us to the transcendental Brahman.

Thus we find that Mother Kali stands for a glorified being, a Mother who is intent upon giving deliverance from delusion. It is in this aspect that the lover of the Mother worships Her as Kali. He calls upon Her: "Oh compassionate Mother! I am at the mercy of this all-powerful mind. I am tyrannised by the ego and the senses. I have become enslaved by the Shad-Ripus and this whole army of Vasanas, Vrittis and Samskaras. They are ever battling against me. Therefore, Thou alone can'st save me from these terrible foes." He invokes Her aid and power to help destroy all these factors, so that when he cannot battle and overcome them, he gets the strength of the Mother and She graciously comes to his aid and in Her symbolically terrible form She helps him overcome the senses and attain mastery and victory over the mind.

This indeed is the content of the Durga Saptashati, the scripture which we read during these nine days. It contains thirteen chapters which describe this process of the Mother giving battle to, on behalf of divine beings, and destroys the entire array of cosmic nescience, of wickedness, of all that is a negation of the Supreme Truth. Each aspect of this negation of truth is depicted in this great scripture which is a wonderful allegory, by some particular demon; and these demons are given appropriate names and forms according to those aspects of nescience. And the thirteen chapters describe how Mother using numerous forms annihilates all the aspects of evil, of nescience, ignorance and this cosmic delusion. And at the end the Supreme Victory to the powers of wisdom and knowledge is achieved and the Jiva is freed for ever from ignorance.

This is not peculiar to the Shakti cult or Devi-worshippers. We will find this allegory in all the religions of the world. We have God and Satan in Christian theology; Satan represents the antithesis of all that is divine, all that is of Light. We have the Ariman and Ahura Mazda in the Zoroastrian religion; and in that religion Ariman stands for forces corresponding to the conception of Satan in Christianity. We have the Mara in Buddhism. Even so we have in Hinduism the force of evil, call it Maya, ignorance or Asuric forces, which stand for all that is the antithesis of light, knowledge, wisdom and Atman. They are called in Vedantic parlance the Anatman, to be overcome by the Knowledge of Atma. That is the central theme of this great scripture—the Saptashati—where Mother enables Her sons to do away with Evil with the help of Her aspect as Mother Kali.

दुर्गे स्मृता हरसि भीतिमशेषजन्तोः
स्वस्थैः स्मृता मतिमतीव शुभां ददासि
दारिद्र्यदुःखभयहारिणि का त्वदन्या
सर्वोपकारकरणाय सदाऽऽर्द्रचित्ता

ॐ दुं दुर्गायै नमः

DESTRUCTION: THE SPRINGBOARD TO CONSTRUCTION

या देवी सर्वभूतेषु श्रद्धारूपेण संस्थिता ।
नमस्तस्यै नमस्तस्यै नमस्तस्यै नमो नमः ॥

SALUTATIONS again and again to the blessed aspect as Durga, Kali the Terrible. Now try to see Divine Mother, the ultimate Goal and Destination of all spiritual aspiration, the Divine Mother who is one with the Para Brahman, Who is the origin and support and ultimate destination of all creation.

We have dwelt yesterday upon Mother in Her aspect as Durga, Kali the Terrible, and tried to see and understand how beneath Her terrible exterior and how within Her drama of apparent destruction, She is in reality the all-compassionate and all-benign Mother who destroys in order to build, who takes away in order to give in abundance, and who is in reality the one who ultimately reveals Herself to us as the Light of lights, the Eternal Light of the Atman, after having helped us annihilate the dense darkness of ignorance.

The very conception of the name Durga, the Mother in Her apparently terrible and destructive aspect, is a significant thing to be understood. In the Saptashati the origin of the name Durga has been given in one verse where we have it described that She, who saves us from all that is calamitous, She who saves us from danger and trouble, is known as Durga. Because She saves Her devotees from all sorrows, dangers and calamities, She is called Devi Durga. She being conceived of in this peculiar aspect of an all-destroying power is not only capable of being esoterically interpreted and explained that She destroys all that is undesirable but also it is based upon universal experience.

Life Involves Destruction

We find that this entire world and the life of man is pervaded by destruction. Without destruction there can be no life. The destruction is ultimately a part of a continuous constructive process. This philosophy of destruction can be realised even through an observation and a study of man's everyday life. *Annagatah Pranah* refers to man's life which is founded upon physical body. If we withdraw this food, man's body cannot last. Let us take this process of nourishing the body and keeping up life. The very process of producing food is based upon a continuous series of destruction. We have first of all—if we desire to cultivate grain—to destroy all thorns, weeds and jungle-growth upon the surface of the earth. Then we have to break the surface of the earth and we have the implements which are driven into the earth; the earth is, as it

were, wounded. Then we have to sow the seed which
dies in order that it may sprout forth into a plant. This
process of destruction continues when the grain is
produced. We have to husk it. It destroys the outer
covering, then the grain is got. If it is to be converted
into food, we have to destroy trees for timber with the
cruel axe. This firewood in its turn has got to immo-
late itself in the flame. Thus destroying itself, it gives
up heat and thus the food is cooked. Upon the table
man destroys the food. The form, the shape and the
nature of the food are destroyed. Until it reaches his
body and manifests there as vitality, a series of the
process of destruction has got to go on. This is only
one typical instance. Like that we may observe any
part of man's life upon earth; and we will find that
whatever is built is based upon a series of apparent
destructions. The sum-total of it is found to achieve
the desired result of ultimate construction.

Upon a much larger scale also we find that this
process is inevitable for the very sustenance of life
upon earth. If the process of destruction of the human
body at death were no to be, then we would never
need a Malthus to confront us with the frightful
theory that there would not be enough space or food
to house and feed the overpopulated earth. Overpopulation is a terrible spectre which is not visible to
the ordinary layman; but to the economist and the
politician who have got a world-view of things. Overpopulation is a constant menace to mankind. It is the
institution of this destructive aspect of the Mother as
death and annihilation of the physical body that keeps

the spectre of overpopulation at bay and also saves mankind. In spite of this, when the population on earth far exceeds the capacity of man to produce the necessities of life, a situation is there before mankind which makes him tremble, a situation which baffles the politician and the economist. There again steps in the Benign Power of the all-compassionate and loving Mother in Her destructive aspect. Man does not know how to stem this tide of menacing overpopulation; She manifests as an earth-quake, as a war, as a widespread famine, as floods, as epidemic the cosmic aspect.

Therefore, we find in all processes of human life if each of the several processes is taken, by itself, we find that even the most constructive process is nothing but an ultimate culmination of a series of necessary and inevitable destructive processes—destructive as conceived by man. To the ordinary mind destruction usually implies the removal of anything from existence, a thing that is, when destroyed, ceases to be. This philosophy of the ceasing to be in one form and developing or progressing into another form is the very basis for this conception of the Mother as the all-destroying Durga or Kali. It is this philosophy of destruction that is ultimately found to be a philosophy of transcendence. It is the outcome, the necessity, of transcending the lower, if we have to reach the higher. It is a process of destroying the gross in order that scope may be given for the manifestation of the subtle. We have to destroy darkness if light has to come in. We have to transcend impurity, if we have to reach purify. Imperfection is destroyed if perfection is to be gained. Even so the lesser is destroyed to give place to the greater.

Not Destruction but Transcendence

Thus destruction upon the spiritual level ultimately comes to express itself as a positive transcendence where a series of progressive constructions are undertaken, by a series of destruction of each lower form so that it may give place to each succeeding form higher than itself. Thus, we see that this process of transcending is a desideratum and not something to be shirked; for as long as we are clinging to the lower, as long as we refuse to let the lower go, we will not be able to attain the higher. It is the intervention of the divine power in this aspect of destroying lower that makes it possible for the attainment of the higher. As today we are to specially consider this application of Mother in Her aspect of Durga or the all-compassionate Kali to the specific process of Yoga and Sadhana, we shall see how Mother is to manifest Herself in the individual personality of the seeker, in what way is the Sadhaka to invoke and to make manifest the Divine Mother within himself if She is to be a tangible and helpful force in the progress of his Yoga Sadhana. In trying to consider this, we will do well to first of all get an idea of what this process of Yoga Sadhana. In trying to consider this, we will do well to first of all get an idea of what this process of Yoga Sadhana actually implies.

Yoga Sadhana is as we all know a process of the human being transcending the imperfections and limitations, defects, weaknesses and impurities of his limited, finite, human nature and ascending upward into and partaking of the infinite, eternal, divine consciousness. In setting about to do this through the path of Yoga and spiritual life, man is confronted with a peculiar situation, a problem. It is not as though he has merely to take a single step from his human nature to divine nature; because when he sets about this task, he finds that inherent in his human nature, there is a whole range of qualities that are essentially subhuman. This is explained in a special manner which is peculiar to the Hindu culture. The theory of re-incarnation has laid down that the Jiva has arrived at the stage of man after having gone through a long series of transmigrations, through numerous lower births from the most elementary forms of the minerals and the plant and the primary forms of life like the amoeba. During this process of passing through various lower stages of life, his consciousness acquires the impression of the predominant traits of each one of these birth phases. Therefore, when he arrives at the human stage, in addition to this quality of human intelligence, the power of thought and discrimination, he has also a whole host of previously-acquired tendencies and characteristics which belong to the subhuman plane. Therefore, we find in him such qualities which are usually attributed to particular types of animal—the cunningness of the fox, the cruelty of the tiger, the venomousness of the scorpion and the lethargy of the lower species of creatures, the gluttony of the pig, and all the evil qualities which are not to be classed as human. These form part of the nature of man though he has risen above the bestial kingdom. Man is thus a brute endowed with a higher capacity of discrimination, knowledge, thinking, etc. Therefore, we find that the human being is a triune being. He is as it were midway between the beast-world and the God-world. There is the brutal nature on the one side of him. There is the divine nature upon the other side of him. In between he finds himself sometimes swayed by the bestial instincts on him—as lethargy, passion, cruelty, anger; and sometimes raised up, at rare moments, to sublime heights where he manifests divine qualities like compassion, justice, truth, purity and so on.

Sacrifice the Beast in You

The Sadhak's task is, therefore, to first and foremost entirely eradicate all that is gross, all that is animalistic, brutal and beastly in his nature. These qualities have to be thoroughly overhauled and taken out of his nature. After this process is done, the transformation of the human nature has to be taken in hand and it has to be sublimated, and transformed into a higher divine nature. It is precisely this study of man as a composite being containing the lower animalistic nature and then the human nature endowed with discrimination, consciousness of higher ideals of a noble divine purpose of this human birth upon this earth, and the capacity to actually rise up into a higher divine consciousness—it is this study of man and this knowledge of the nature of man that has led to the conception of the animal sacrifice as also the Narabali which later on became degenerated into the actual outward practice of sacrificing animals at the altar of Mother Kali. What was an idealistic conception to symbolise a certain inward process in man's spiritual life later on became externalised in a degenerate form in the shape of the practice of animal sacrifice. For what the animal sacrifice to be done to the deity Kali symbolised was the invoking of this divine power in Its destructive aspect as Durga or Kali, within the personality of the seeker so that this divine power may work within the aspirant and completely annihilate the beast within the man. This sacrifice of the lower self of the seeker, of the animal nature of the Sadhaka is what is achieved by Mother Durga or Kali in the first stages of an aspirant's Sadhana-life.

To this end, the aspirant has first to analyse and try to ascertain what are the prominent aspects in which the animal side of his lower nature has its play in his present personality. One may be a slave to anger more than to anything else; another lust, to carnality; and a third one to some other aspect. One may find several aspects are dominant in his lower personality and holding him slave. It may be that at different times different passions get the upper hand. He has, therefore, to first of all introspect, analyse himself and try to find out what particular manifestation of the gross lower Gunas are operating within his nature. A sincere study of one's own nature is absolutely indispensable to the Sadhaka. Unless he knows what is there in him that is undesirable, inimical to success in Yoga, that stands as obstacle to Sadhana, it is not possible for him to proceed correctly upon this difficult inward Path of Yoga. More difficult is it because these dark aspects of the gross part of man's nature, of the Tamo-Guna are not always clearly expressed and visible within himself. Far more easy it is to fight the external foes, because you know what they are and their nature and strength so that you can meet them on their own level. The inner enemies of man—anger, lust, jealousy, hatred, cruelty, etc.,—have various forms and are invisible; they are cloaked under various disguises and unless the seeker invokes the grace of Antaryamin or the Indwelling Presence of the Divine in him, to aid him, it will be a difficult tak for him to proceed with this process of destroying his lower, selfish, egoistic nature. To analyse another person is an easier matter because you can observe his outward behaviour, etc., but this self-analysis is a very difficult task—first, because of the basic extrovert tendency of the human mind—it tends to go outward to the objects of the universe and to make it go inward is itself a delicate task; secondly man is prevented by the ego-sense from finding out and knowing what is defective, what is bad, that which is not gratifying to the ego. It is common experience that that which is not pleasant to the ego is hidden from its gaze. Therefore, it is difficult of self-analysis, and this is one of the reasons why in the Eastern mode of spiritual life the aspirant is asked to go and submit himself to a Guru. He approaches the Guru, surrenders himself to the Guru and tries to live with the Guru so that the defects and undesirable qualities within him which he will not be able to perceive by his own efforts, by his own study of himself, can be easily perceived by the Guru and then the Guru puts the aspirant in such situations where he will be able to overcome these defects and also sometimes gives him such tasks where the eradication of these qualities becomes absolutely necessary; and he may also give the aspirant specific instructions and where necessary even admonish him so that these hidden defects, hidden to the aspirant but not hidden from the gaze of the Guru, its destruction becomes facilitated. Thus the Guru also fulfils to a great extent the role of Mother Kali in helping the aspirant to destroy the vicious tendencies and evil traits that are the stumbling blocks in the very first stages of one's spiritual life.

Manifestations of Durga in Spiritual Sadhana

Mother Durga thus manifests Herself in and through the form of the Guru, in the form of an aspirant in the aspirant himself to rise to a higher plane, in the form of a ruthless self-criticism and a self-examination; and when this analysis reveals to the seeker the picture of his lower animalistic self in all its detail then the Mother has to be invoked by him as a strong resolution and a strong determination to completely root out these evil tendencies because this aspct of the Mother is absolutely necessary if one has to start progressing upon the path of Yoga. To be unaware of the defects is the first great obstacle; and then if we get over this and become aware of our defects, but if we do not do anything about them in spite of our knowing our defects, the defects will remain and we will not progress. The next stage is, we must have a fiery determination and a strong power of will to completely break down this lower nature within us. Once this determination is invoked, the Mother manifests Herself as a strong will-power and a resoluteness in the aspirant to conquer and attain victory over his animalistic nature.

Next She has to manifest Herself in dynamic will. This will has to be translated into dynamic action, as Sadhana-Sakti, in the aspirant, so that day by day he begins to fight these evil tendencies in all moments of his daily life, in his actions, in his dealings with others, in his thoughts and motives and in his attitudes; this is done by the Sadhana-Sakti aspect of the Divine-Mother. Thus the Sadhana must proceed. For doing his task successfully he has to generate the power of the Divine Mother as Sadhana-Sakti and all the different processes of Yoga. If he is prey to certain lower appetites, he has to completely destroy those appetites, by a series of Sadhanas like Tapascharya, leaving off certain things, denying himself the gratification of those appetites.

It may be said that the denial of certain appetites may drive them underground as it were, to overcome man at some propitious moment, in the form of temptations. Here we have to put forward a certain great truth. It has been found out that to try to overcome an appetite by feeding it is the most impossible thing upon earth; because sense-cravings are likened to a huge conflagration or fire—and if we try to satisfy them, they say, this process acts as ghee poured into the fire. So that we actually give it something to consume; and by consuming it the fire blazes forth all the stronger and more furiously. It is on the other hand, by withdrawing the food to this blaze of sense-cravings that they die a natural death. Therefore, Tapascharya is another form in which Mother Durga manifests Herself in the aspirant.

In order to bear the rigour of Tapascharya, one must develop the power of Titiksha, the power of enduring things which may be very unpleasant and which may be very difficult and undesirable to the lower side of man. Titiksha in its various forms like fasting, vigil, etc., and self-denial in its various forms like giving up those things which the mind likes best for some period of time, e.g., saltless diet, taking tea without sugar, non-using shoes, come under this category. Methods by which we check some natural downward tendency and control some sensual appetite which draws the personality towards the objective world, have to be intelligently thought over and thus a whole programme of Sadhana has to be worked out by every individual Sadhaka or spiritual aspirant. It is the sum-total of these expressions of the Mother in the Sadhaka that ultimately enable him to transcend the first stage of spiritual life and Sadhana and completely attain victory over the lower nature in him.

Thus, the animal sacrifice, as it were, is achieved through the invocation of the divine Power within us in its evil-destroying, darkness-annihilating, and Tamas-overcoming aspect. This is the significance and meaning of the worship of Mother Kali in the spiritual life of the aspirant.

It is impossible for anyone to cover the entire field of the manifestation of the Mother in Her aspect as Durga in the life of the aspirant. It is naturally a process which each one has to think out and work out for himself. It is only in its general form that we can say that Mother has to be manifested in the form of a ruthless self-analysis, a firm determination and a dynamic attempt to give expression to this resolution and the qualities like austerity, endurance, self-denial, fasting and the various other aspects of Yoga Sadhana, that we will be able to give it while dealing with the question in a general way.

Saptashati's Lesson

Next, we have to transcend even the human nature with all its wrong conceptions and with its ego-sense, if we are to reach the higher divine consciousness. This process of overcoming even the human side of the aspirant's consciousness is symbolised by human sacrifice or Narabali. The arrangement of the Saptashati in the three aspects of first the killing of Madhu-Kaitabha, secondly the killing of Mahishasura, and thirdly the killing of the brothers Shumbha and Nishumbha with their host of demons, symbolises the different stages of Sadhana. Madhu and Kaitabha represent the gross form of the lower nature of man. Mahishasura represents the next stage, the annihilation of the Rajo-Guna aspect. When we come to the third part, we find the Asura is a far finer type of demon; he is a king, very wealthy, greatly cultured, but with a supervening vanity. He possesses dominance over all the celestial hosts and he possesses the entire wealth of the world. Everything that is desirable, all that is best in all the fourteen worlds, are possessed by the invincible brothers and they command a huge host of warriors. One of the warriors is a demon called Raktabija who is equated with the human egoism. It is after the destruction of egoism in its lower form that the ultimate destruction of Shumbha and Nishumbha is possible, symbolising as it were the destruction of Vikshepa and Avarana Shaktis, by which the last barrier between the human and the Divine is removed and the culmination of the Sadhak's spiritual life is achieved through the grace of the Mother, with the attainment of identification with the Cosmic Supreme Being.

भवानि त्वं दासे मयि वितर दृष्टिं सकरुणा-
मिति स्तोतुं वाञ्छन् कथयति भवानी त्वमिति चः ।
तदैव त्वं तस्मै दिशसि निजसायुज्यपदवीं
मुकुन्दब्रह्मेन्द्रस्फुटमकुटनीराजितपदाम् ॥

FOURTH NIGHT

LAKSHMI: THE SUPREME SUSTAINER

सर्वमंगलमांगल्ये शिवे सर्वार्थसाधिके ।
शरण्येत्र्यंबके देवि नारायणि नमोऽस्तु ते ॥

SALUTATIONS to the blessed Source, destination of all! Salutations to the Supreme Power of the Almighty Being manifest as Saraswati! Salutations to the Power manifest as Mahalakshmi and that Primal Power manifest as Durga!

Today is the fourth day of the worship of the Godhead conceived as the Mother of all creation. From today we enter into the next phase of this deeply significant adoration of the Mother, in Her aspect of the nourishing and sustaining function of the Supreme Shakti. From today for three days all over India the Mother will be adored as Mahalakshmi. The last three days will be Her worship in Her aspect of Mahasaraswati, culminating on the tenth day, the Vijaya Dasami.

Involution of Spirit in Matter

When we take up the consideration of this peculiar arrangement of the Navaratra Puja, the worship of the Mother in the three aspects, in this particular order of Durga, Lakshmi and Saraswati, we are confronted with a very significant truth. It is in itself the revelation of a certain actual law. We know when the transcendent power which is unmanifest and beyond all names and forms becomes manifest as the visible universes, as phenomena and takes on the appearance of Nama-Rupa, there commences a process of involution, of the transcendent becoming relative, of the nameless and formless entering into forms and we see in it a process of the supreme, subtlest of the subtle, the original cause and source becoming progressively grosser and grosser until it reaches the ultimate grossest manifestation in its termination as inert matter. This process of involution is the order of the projection of phenomena. It is the order of one becoming the many, the unmanifest becoming the manifest, the cause appearing as the various effects. Correspondingly, when from this movement into matter the seeker strives to rise back into the original state of transcendence, through a reverse process of an inner movement from matter back into the spirit, we find that the manifestation of this divine power or Shakti starts operating in exactly the contrary and opposite way. When involution starts, it is first the creativity of Brahma that begins to operate. The creative power functions and names and forms stream forth from the great Prakriti. From the state of being beyond, when the names and forms stream forth in the realm of Maya, these names and forms come under the sway of time,

under the threefold aspect of the past, the present and
the future. As they have to retain their names and
forms and exist in threefold time, there arises the
function of the preservative, the sustaining, the
nourishing and the protecting factor. Mahashakti then
operates as the dynamic counterpart of Vishnu the
Preserver, He who sustains and keeps up the world-
process. She is Maha-Lakshmi. Change has to take
place and names and forms are in their very nature
perishable and passing because they come under the
operation of time or Kala. This process of breaking up
the names and forms is performed by Rudra who
presides over Laya or dissolution. Thus these functions
operate—starting with creativity, then sustenance and
then dissolution. This is the descent into matter.

The Evolution of Man to Godhead

But, as it has been said in the Gita: to the man
of the spirit everything operates in exactly the opposite direction as it does to the man of the world
who is immersed in matter. That which is day to the
man of the world is night to the man of the spirit and
to those things to which the man of the world is
awake as it were in his perception the man of the
spirit is asleep and does not recognise them. To those
things to which the man of the world is asleep in his
perception to all those higher things of the spirit, the
man of God is fully awake. What the worldly man perceives the Yogi turns away from and does not perceive; what the worldly man fails to perceive the Yogi
perceives in his state of spiritual awakening. In accordance with this law, when the self-same divine power

begins to act in the inner realm of the spiritual ascent in the realm of evolution as opposed to involution, the seeker adores the power in a contrary way. He first invokes the Mother in Her destructive aspect so that She has to destroy the whole of matter which is upon the Jiva having involved into grossness, having involved into matter, having become immersed in nescience; therefore, the first process is to break free from the grip of matter, to shatter the shackles of nescience and delusion and to attain victory over that which is gross and to rise up into the realm of the pure, the subtle and the spiritual. First Mother in Her aspect of the Power and Force to destroy the grossness and the influence of the material world is invoked; and then when one rises up into the path of Yoga and spiritual life it is Mother as Lakshmi who is invoked next so that She may bestow upon him all that is necessary to sustain the spiritual life, whereas in the involution She becomes necessary to sustain the material life and to protect and preserve the life in this external physical world of matter. We have to remember that the Motherhood of God is always conceived of as the twofold Shaktis, Vidya-Maya and Avidya-Maya. It is in this aspect of Vidya-Maya She now comes to be adored and invoked by the seeker and therefore Lakshmi in Her aspect as Vidya-Maya sustains, nourishes, protects and preserves the seeker's spiritual ascent, his Yoga and his Sadhana.

When he passes on still higher beyond the path of Yoga, he invokes the great Mother in Her aspect as the first emanation from the transcendence of

Supreme Being, which is nearest to that, and in Her aspect as Mahasaraswati She is the first emanation and She is the bestower of Knowledge. She makes the Jiva unite with the Paramatma or Para Brahman and attain the universal cosmic consciousness, the consciousness of the Infinite Atma. It is in Her aspect as Vidya-Maya that the seeker worships the Mother in exactly the reverse way so that She may achieve for him the return back from matter into the original state of Pure Spirit.

The Eightfold Lakshmi

When we come first of all to consider Maha Lakshmi in Her cosmic aspect as Avidya-Maya who has to preserve the world-process which has involved out of the Supreme Being, we find that She is con- ceived of as all the various things that are necessary to have a prosperous and successful life upon this earthplane. We have the conception of Mahalakshmi in Her eightfold forms and the Hindus refer to Her as the Ashta-Lakshmi. For the sustenance of life upon this earth the most important thing is food. All beings live upon this physical plane through the nourishment derived from physical food and the chief source of food upon earth is corn that is cultivated. Grain is *Dhaanya*. Therefore, Mother is worshipped as Dhaa- nya-Lakshmi. It is a common sight to see upon a par- ticular day in the year set apart for this specific purpose, the cultivator and all the people worshipping the freshly-cut sheaves of golden corn that has been gathered at harvest-time. It is a very joyous festival. The first crop of golden corn which has filled the field is cut, taken up with great ceremony, with music and rejoicing and it is brought to the house wherein all the ceremonial worship due to a deity is offered to it. Thus Mother in Her universal aspect as life-sustaining corn is regarded as the most important factor and in this form Lakshmi is manifest in this world of ours.

Secondly, for all human dealings, in society, both intra-national and international, money or wealth is of paramount importance. Without wealth man cannot live with happiness, prosperity and success. He cannot undertake any works; and therefore, Mother is also conceived of as *Dhana*. It means wealth in any form—in the form of coins, goods—all valuable things. Thus wealth also is revered and worshipped in society.

The Mother in these various forms is worshipped by different classes of people in India. The Hindu society is based upon the beautiful plan of Varnashrama. There is a general division of labour in the whole society as it is and different aspects of national life are entrusted to different sections of the community and in Her eightfold aspects as Dhaanya-Lakshmi, Dhana-Lakshmi, Dhairya-Lakshmi, Vidya-Lakshmi, Jaya-Lakshmi, Veerya-Lakshmi, Gaja-Lakshmi and Saubhagya-Lakshmi, Mother is worshipped in the form of life-giving corn, of wealth, of Apara-Vidya (knowledge of arts and sciences which is very essential if one must live a civilised and happy life—all knowledge pertaining to this material universe is Mother in the form of Vidya), of Dhairya (to utilise wealth and knowledge one must have enterprise), of Veerya (vitality or virility), of Gaja (royal power or the power of royalty), of Jaya (the power of victory over adverse circumstances, obstacles that stand in the way of a happy, prosperous and successful life) and of Saubhagya (prosperity in general). In these eight aspects, the power of the nourisher and sustainer Lakshmi is manifest in the world of human beings. The Kshatriya worships the Mother in the form of victory-giving weapons; to him the sword and all the other weapons are the victory-giving manifestations of Mahalakshmi. To the Vaishya who belongs to the third social order, who carries on commerce and business in human society, the great power is the power of money; therefore, a day is set apart to specially worship Goddess Lakshmi in this aspect of money, by them. It is a common sight on Deepavali and Lakshmi Puja, especially in wealthy cities like Bombay, when silver coins would be put into a heap and worshipped as any deity would be worshipped by the devout Hindu, as the visible manifestation of Divine Mother Lakshmi Herself. The fourth class, Sudras, worship Lakshmi as grain which they help to produce. By the Brahmin who is the trustee of knowledge and who is to impart knowledge to all people Mother is worshipped in the form of Vidya and as books. Implements of machinery, every sort of Ayudha that help to keep life going upon earth, are also worshipped on Ayudha Puja day. The conception of the Motherhood of God in its aspect as the preserving and life-sustaining form is thus practically demonstrated in the Hindu society in these various ways.

The Sadhak's Attitude to Lakshmi

Thus it is that to the devout Hindu the aspect of the Motherhood as a material power, a power which sustains life upon this physical world is an important aspect of divinity in so far as his material life is concerned and here we have to note that the Hindu shows himself as a sane realist. He realises and accepts the importance and value of the divine power as it is manifest upon the material world in the form of these helpful factors that go to sustain and preserve life for him upon earth in a prosperous and happy state. While we thus recognise his realistic attitude towards the good things of this world, here it will be interesting to note that the Eternal Quest for the Absolute, for the ultimate Being, is also a part and parcel of the consciousness of every true Hindu. The self-same Hindu who devoutly worships the Mother in the form of wealth and all the good things of the world simultaneously admits the fact that once his aspiration for the divine realisation has begun to manifest within himself, this very aspect of Lakshmi which is most important in this work-a-day world of ours has to be resolutely brushed aside, and renounced. Thus he turns his face away from the material things of this world, gives up wealth and takes to the path of renunciation; because he admits that as long as one is deeply concerned with desire and its fulfilment, he has to accept the all-powerful nature of Mother in Her aspect of the things of this world. But the moment he has had enough of these things and he has realised their temporariness, their transience and their perishable nature, and the moment his heart is set upon the eternal thing, he bids adieu to this aspect of the Mother and he invokes the other aspect, viz., the Vidya-Maya. He prays to the Mother that She may release him from the lure and the attraction of Her own deluding power in the form of wealth, prosperity, domestic happiness and all the good things of the world; and thus he makes a deliberate departure from Mother Lakshmi in Her aspect of Avidya. Herein lies the main difference between the man of the world and the seeker. Herein lies the inner significance of the worship fo these two people, of the self-same deity. The man of the world worships the Mother; and at the same time the seeker who has renounced the world also worships Lakshmi. To the surface-observer it would seem that both are carrying on the self-same worship; but once this conception of Lakshmi both in Her Avidya and Vidya aspects is known, then one would see underneath the surface and go beneath the apparent worship, and he will find that for one and the same worship of the self-same deity, Mother Lakshmi, there is a total difference of view or point of approach and the total difference of Bhava or mental attitude between the materialist, a man of desires, and spiritual seeker or the man who has turned away from desire, who has commenced to aspire for the Eternal.

Yet the figure is the same, Mother is the same; and because She is the prosperity-giver and the preserver, the form of Lakshmi is always full of auspiciousness. She is gorgeously dressed. She has got golden ornaments. There is always that symbol of power and pomp, the elephant, which is by Her side. She lives upon a lotus and She holds two lotuses—and these flowers are in full bloom. The significance of these will become apparent when we reflect upon what they stand for. Full-blown lotus represents the fullness in all aspects. Even so, the elephant represents two things: the highest state of prosperity, regal splendour, royal pomp; and at the same time the highest knowledge—elephant represents the fullness of wisdom.

या देवी सर्वभूतेषु लक्ष्मीरूपेण संस्थिता ।
नमस्तस्यै नमस्तस्यै नमस्तस्यै नमो नमः ॥

ॐ श्री महालक्ष्म्यै नमः

THE PATH OF PROSPERITY

सृष्टिस्थितिविनाशानां शक्तिभूते सनातनि ।
गुणाश्रये गुणमये नारायणि नमोऽस्तु ते ॥

SALUTATIONS to the blessed Divine Mother, the life of our lives, the sole support of our existence, the very essence of our being, the inmost core of our consciousness, the goal and ultimate destination of our life, the glorious fruition of our Yoga Sadhana, the Pure Existence-Knowledge and Bliss. We bow to Her again and again as Mother Durga, Lakshmi, and Saraswati. May Her Grace be upon us all.

Mother in Her aspect as Lakshmi is the one great Power upon earth that makes life possible and bearable here. Were it not for blessed Mother Lakshmi, life upon earth would be a journey of sorrows and pain. It will be a vale of tears; for due to the transient nature of things and due to the all-pervasive aspect of Mother Durga, destruction is ever haunting the footsteps of the Jiva from the moment it sees the light of day upon earth until it reaches the grave. Verily, life on earth is a life of pain and death.

It is the shining, radiant and joy-giving aspect of Lakshmi Devi that makes life bearable by balancing the pain and destruction that pervades this earthly existence with the sweet elements of light, love, rejoicing, prosperity and happiness in all its various forms. Mother pervades all aspects of human life as auspiciousness. She is Kalyani. She is Mangalam. She is Saubhagyavati. Both in the wider sphere of national life as well as in the intimate sphere of a being's domestic circle, Mother manifests Herself in all Her radiance and good cheer so that life is sustained through Her light, through Her charm, and Her Grace. Thus, Mother Durga and Mother Lakshmi keep up the balance in this Samsaric life and make it possible for the Jiva to forget the harsh realities of this transitory passing existence and to partake of the good things of life with some extent of joy.

Signs of National Glory

It is a very interesting and very useful task to try to be aware of the Divine Mother as Lakshmi in both these spheres so that we shall be in a position consciously to work towards the maintenance of the presence of Mother Lakshmi in these spheres by doing which we shall be able to fill this terrestrial life with happiness and prosperity. In the wider sphere of man's social and national life, Mother appears as those modes which counteract and counter-balance the terrible modes of the divine Shakti in its aspects as Durga Devi. We have seen how in order to sustain the very life upon earth Durga manifests Herself in aspects of very necessary destructivity and annihilation, how but for Her benign breaking down process, life upon earth would end in absolute chaos and ruin, catastrophe and calamity. Thus in Her terrible aspects as war, epidemics, famine, natural catastrophies like flood, fire, earthquake, Mother Durga destroys in order to save, in order to see that life continues. Lakshmi Devi manifests in this life as modes which counterbalance and counteract this activity of Her own aspect as Durga, by appearing as peace instead of war,—when Lakshmi is propitious there is peace in the universe, peace amongst nations and mankind, and there is freedom from all civil strife—as plenty, fertility, abundant harvest and, as the counterpart of disease and epidemics, Lakshmi graces society in the form of health, well-being, welfare of the children and of the women, and of a good standard of the nation's health. In Her aspects as the preservative forces like the medical profession, hospitals, the fire brigade, police, etc, the power of Vishnu-Shakti, Divine Mother Lakshmi, appears to counteract the calamities of nature and to protect the life and welfare of men and their properties. Therefore, to the politician, to the administrator, to the leaders of society, these aspects are the signs of Lakshmi being present in the social structure.

Where these things are neglected, we find that the happiness of the people is destroyed. Their progress is arrested; and prosperity leaves that nation and that society. Therefore, the ancient law-givers laid down that every true administrator must have in mind these aspects of the Mother and he should always diligently try to see that he does what all he can in order to increase these factors in society, through which Mother Lakshmi manifests Herself and in which this benign progressive aspect of Vishnu-Shakti dwells. Temples, schools, playgrounds, parks, flower-gardens, tanks—all these factors in human society are so many manifestations of the Vishnu-Shakti. They are all Mother Lakshmi being visible through these symbols. Therefore, we find that in this land of Dharma, Bharatavarsha, there will be no place without a temple. It may be the most insignificant village, a mere hamlet, with a handful of houses; yet without even the dignity of a pucca structure, at least under the shade of some tree there will be a village deity that is worshipped by that community. Where there is a village without place of worship, there no religious man will set foot. They will say: "This place has no Lakshmi therein." They will avoid such a place. Where there is no good provision for water, for people and cattle to drink, there people will say that Lakshmi does not dwell; and holy men will turn away from such a place. All Dharmic people, people of wealth, ever tried to utilise their God-given wealth for setting up these visible expressions of Lakshmi throughout the land. To plant trees, to dig wells and tanks, to donate gardens and playgrounds, to build new temples where there are none and to renovate old temples which had fallen into disrepair, and to start choultries where travellers may come and rest themselves, to have feeding houses where weary pilgrims, holy men, men of God, mendicants and the religious students may get food—all these were considered and even now they are considered to be works of Dharma, of great merit, which will bless the giver with happiness here and hereafter. Education also was a visible expression of Lakshmi in Her aspect as Vidya-Lakshmi which is one of the eight aspects of Ashta-Lakshmi. Thus the expression of Mother Lakshmi in all these forms was regarded by our law-givers as something which every man, every citizen should try to increase in the country and in the society so that a state of prosperity may always prevail in the land.

The Foremost Duty of National Leaders

It will do well for all the leaders of men in whichever country or nation they may be and to all social leaders and administrators, to bear in mind that the increase and the preservation of these aspects of Lakshmi in society is not only one of the primary concerns and duties, but also to preserve and increase all these factors contained in it the seeds of enduring welfare and happiness of all people. Thus, as long as man was still conscious of the reality of this world, as long as he felt the reality of these external things, it was his duty to see that he did not neglect any of these factors. A false assimilation of the Hindu religion, and wrong conception of man's duty or rather an indigestion of the Vedantic food from the Upanishads, had led to an unfortunate neglect of this factor of realism in the Hindu race in centuries gone by so that having half-assimilated notions of Vairagya, of God-realisation and of the unreality of the world, the Indians as a whole became apathetic towards the preservation of these aspects of Mahalakshmi, thinking that all these things were only in the realm of Maya and they were not worthwhile giving one's attention to; and to turn away from them in a sort of so-called lofty other-worldliness was the acme of philosophic life of wisdom. The Hindu nation had to pay a terrible price for having this sort of apathy towards Mother in Her aspects of Lakshmi in this external world and the price was losing Her in some of Her most precious aspects, viz., freedom, prosperity and national self-respect. Thus, Lakshmi left the Hindu nation when their mistaken notions of philosophy made the majority of people neglect Her and discard Her worship in the form of a robust realism and in the form of a practical idealism in this external life. Therefore, education was neglected and all these social works were neglected as something belonging to the realm of ignorance which it was not worthwhile to pursue; and even while man was firmly bound up in body-consciousness upon the gross plane, he shut his eyes to the realities of this physical world and tried to dispense with all these things with the declaration that they were all only transitory and evanescent. Thus, a state of Tamas supervened which was opposed to Lakshmi and therefore two centuries of slavery was the result—slavery to those who were better worshippers of Lakshmi in the real sense of the term in the external world. They, the British people, were able to propitiate Her and thus all that was best in Bharatavarsha, all the prosperity-giving elements went over to the West where, though they were materialists yet they worshipped Lakshmi.

When saints and great thinkers of modern India realised that it was the neglect of Lakshmi through a succumbing to Tamas that was at the root of the Indian problem, they at once gave a dynamic social philosophy to the Hindu nation. The clarion call for the Hindu nation to wake up from its slumber of Tamo-Guna and to plunge into selfless service and to vigorously take life with a realistic attitude and point of view was sounded by these great modern saviours of India. Thus a revival came about and the half-assimilated and wrong notions of philosophy were driven out from the heads of the people and they were taught how one has to be a dynamic worshipper as long as his body is still a very real thing to him and as long as he has not risen to that state of consciousness, of spiritual evolution, when he would be able to actually feel within the heart of hearts that the world is but a passing dream and that the unmanifest alone is the actual reality. This is a mistake which it is very easy to fall into, to think that one has risen very high upon the spiritual plane and to neglect the things which ought not to be neglected in the beginning stages of one's evolution. In the beginning these things which may later on have to be renounced and given up, themselves form the first stepping-stones upon which one has to rise higher and higher. Thus the apathy due to Tamas which was mistakenly considered to be a sort of philosophy and resignation was pointed out and ended and now we are experiencing an era of practical Rajo-Guna where the nation and the Hindu society is being shaken up into wakefulness, into a state of vigorous activity for the good of one and all. This is very happy sign and if this is understood and persisted in the right spirit without allowing the Avidya-Maya of Lakshmi to overshadow our perception and intelligence, it will certainly lead on to the ultimate spiritual evolution which is the real goal of the Hindu nation.

A Stern Warning

Similarly, in the individual's spiritual life, however much it may be true in the ultimate reaches of realisation that he is not this physical body, he is Pure Atman which is beyond body and mind, yet we find that if the aspirant is foolish enough to start with this basis in his life of practical spiritual Sadhana he will come to grief very soon. For the law of this physical world is very exacting and a transgression in this law will at once claim its price. Thus, if one flies away into a Vedantic attitude and neglects his physical body and does not care to maintain its health and give it proper rest or nourishment and thinks he has already attained the consciousness of Atma, he will wake up too late to find out his mistake and he will find that the one superlative instrument of all Yoga Sadhana, viz., this physical body through which one has to do selfless service in order to attain the much-desired purity of heart and character, becomes damaged beyond repair and his progress in Yoga Sadhana becomes severely hampered. In such a case it is only the Grace of the Lord that will have to save him and somehow he will have to make amends for his mistake.

Just as in the individual a neglect of this aspect of the physical factor which may later on have to be transcended brings very undesirable results, even so, in the national life it was necessary to have realised this and to have avoided this degeneracy into Tamas. By the bitter way the Indian society has learnt the lesson and now the very welcome trend of this robust activism, activity based upon Dharma, upon selflessness, motiveless activity, as is now being exemplified by all great leaders, social leaders, political leaders, as well as spiritual leaders like our Gurudev, has now created a new constructive wave in the society and this nation, which augurs well for our ultimate rising up into the realm of Saraswati, where through this activity a state of peace, prosperity, national health and well-being, national literacy and higher education of all people will come into existence and through this a national spiritual regeneration will be made possible. For, without the widespread manifestation of Lakshmi in the society and the nation there can be no hope of the manifestation of the Goddess Saraswati in Her aspect of higher spiritual knowledge coming into existence, because as they have said, religion cannot be preached to hungry stomachs and bare backs.

Therefore, we have first of all to have a realistic approach to this problem of national and social life. We must give to the nation and to people those aspects of Lakshmi by which alone they will live a life of health, of well-being, and in such a state of all-round prosperity, literacy and health, higher aspirations will begin to sprout up. These aspirations are there; but they are all dormant and due to the absence of Lakshmi in the land and in the society the aspirations are given no chance to manifest themselves in the heart of man; for, poverty stultifies all higher aspirations and when hunger pinches man's stomach there can be no thought of higher idealism.

Therefore, this very great and significant importance of the visible manifestation of Lakshmi or Vishnu-Shakti in the life of every race and nation has to be recognised upon its own merits, with discrimination and Vairagya, and through Lakshmi one must approach Saraswati which is the ultimate aim of the Bharatiya Samskriti.

या श्रीः स्वयं सुकृतिनां भवनेष्वलक्ष्मी
पापात्मनां कृतधियां हृदयेषु बुद्धिः ।
श्रद्धा सतां कुलजनप्रभवस्य लज्जा
तां त्वां नताः स्म परिपालय देवि विश्वम् ॥

ॐ महालक्ष्म्यै च विद्महे विष्णुपत्न्यै च धीमहि तन्नो लक्ष्मी: प्रचोदयात् ।

GODDESS OF AUSPICIOUSNESS AT HOME AND AT HEART

शरणागतदीनार्तपरित्राणपरायणे
सर्वस्यार्तिहरे देवि ! नारायणि ! नमोऽस्तु ते ।

SALUTATIONS crores of times to the blessed Divine Mother who is the one Power that sustains the universe. She is the source of Power manifest in and through the various names and forms. Salutations again and again to Her who manifests within our hearts as aspiration, as Sadhana-Shakti and preserves our Yoga and who ultimately manifests Herself as Pure Knowledge in our consciousness and illuminates our entire being.

Today we come to the third sacred day of worship of the Divine Mother in Her aspect of Sri Lakshmi or Vishnu Shakti or Narayani. On this sixth day of the Navaratra Worship ours is the rare blessing and good fortune to dwell upon the Goddess Lakshmi as She manifests to the individual in the intimate sphere of the home, the domestic sphere, at heart in Her very important and significant inner aspect as the Daivi Sampat which are developed in the personality of the seeker and Sadhaka and the Mumukshu. In these two aspects She is of a special and practical importance to us all in as much as knowing the Mother in these aspects we shall be able to recognise both Her presence and Her absence as such, and by recognising which we shall be able to strive to preserve those aspects in which She is present and try to cultivate and bring into manifestation and expression those aspects of Hers which we may find to be absent.

Glorious Indian Womanhood

In the domestic sphere the conception of the Goddess Lakshmi is wonderful and unique in this blessed land of Bharatavarsha. For the home itself is regarded as the Abode of Lakshmi where the Mother manifests Herself in the worshipful form of the Grihini. Therefore, we are familiar with the expression Grihalakshmi, the Mother who presides over the auspiciousness, welfare and progress of the home-life and family. She is conceived of as the very embodiment of Goddess Lakshmi. Herein we have a unique feature of the Bharatiya Samskriti which is a thing that is found to be absent in the West. In the West the woman is more conceived of as the wife, an equal partner to the man vying for privilege with him in all spheres of activity and trying to assert not only her equality but even further her personal independence. Whereas, to the Hindu heart woman is the mother. It is the motherhood of the woman that is ever present in the consciousness of the true Hindu. This is the blessing of being born in this Punya-Bhumi for out of this conception we shall be enabled to rise to the realisation of the Motherhood of God. This Matri-Bhav or the attitude and the vision of woman as the Mother is a means of purifying our hearts and minds and elevating us to a higher state wherein the descent of divine light becomes facilitated.

Thus, home is the abode of Lakshmi, to the Hindu; therefore, every home in Hindu society is a temple of auspiciousness, of Mangalya, presided over by Lakshmi in and through the pure person of the Grihalakshmi. The greatness, the power and the radiance of the Mother as embodied in the mother of the home is the radiance of chastity, Pativrata Dharma, which forms the grandeur, the glory and the inner radiance of the Grihalakshmi. To her it is the power that is unsurpassed in the whole world. The entire conception of Dharma for women may be summed up in this single word Pativratya. To the Grihalakshmi in her sphere of the home, the husband or the Patidev is what to the Sadhaka and the seeker in the spiritual life, (in the sphere of Yoga) the Guru is. Even as the Sadhaka looks upon the Guru as the Supreme Being Himself, as identical with God, as brought out in the couplet:

Twam Hi Vishnur Virinchistwam Twam Cha
Devo Maheshwarah
Twameva Shaktiruposi Nirgunastwam Sanatanah

Even so the Patidev is to the wife. Pativratya is the greatest treasure that a woman can possess in this life that makes her not merely an exceptional woman but which makes her a veritable Goddess-upon-earth. For, this power of chastity is the divine element of Goddess Lakshmi Herself. Added to this, the external expression of this internal virtue of chastity, is in the form of modesty. The ornament of the Hindu woman is modesty. She does not care to see others and be seen. This is a craze, a disease, which is developing in the modern era. One likes that the attention of others may be attracted towards oneself; and to this end colourful dresses and every device as invented by the fertile brains of people who are immersed in the deepest of darkness, are utilised so that attention of others may be attracted. This is the direct antithesis or contradiction of the sublime and noble virtue of modesty. If modesty is neglected and this craze for attraction is given place to, then it becomes a denial of Lakshmi Devi. It is Alakshmi. We must always bear in mind that in the eyes of Hindu idealism, modesty is a virtue of paramount importance and in this form the Mother manifests Herself in and through the ideal of noble Indian womanhood.

Lakshmi also manifests Herself in the home in the personality of the Grihalakshmi as grace and sweetness of manners, behaviour and speech. A woman should never be harsh. No harsh word, no rude speech, no hard utterance should ever cross the holy lips of the presiding deity of the Hindu home. This is the ideal, for graciousness and sweetness are a part and parcel of the Hindu conception of the Grihalakshmi. Never to utter harsh words is one of the methods of honouring Lakshmi and worshipping Her.

This is to be borne in mind in all homes; for that alone conduces to real happiness, peace and welfare of the home.

Another custom which is not properly understood is the adornment of the person with two important things, besides the Mangalya-Sutra which is the distinct sign of the Grihalakshmi. In two more aspects Lakshmi is present in the Hindu home; that is in the form of two factors of adornment of the ideal Hindu woman—in the form of flowers and in the form of Tilak. A Hindu woman should never go without the Tilak. There is a special significance and a deep and important reason for the wearing of a sizeable Tilak upon the forehead which is not understood. But it may be accepted without any doubt that there is a very real necessity and importance for this Tilak both from the subjective point of view of the lady wearing it, as also from the objective point of view of all people who have to contact her during Vyavahar. Also, flowers. Flowers are the very manifestation of Lakshmi and they are also to be worn. But, at the same time we should not forget that Mother Lakshmi acts both as the Vidya Maya as also the Avidya Maya. Therefore, in this aspect as the Avidya Maya she is always to be worshipped from a very safe distance and we should daily pray to Her that she may save us from that aspect of Her play and She may only bless us as Her Vidya aspect.

Apart from the manifestations of the Goddess Lakshmi in the person of the Grihalakshmi, She is also manifest as a continuous attitude of worshipfulness to the Patidev and a continuous willing self-sacrificing service of the Lord in and through the husband.

Goddess Lakshmi Herself is the greatest exemplar of this sublime Pati-Seva. For, the Vaishnavite conception of the great Mother is as an Eternal Sevika of the Lord in Vaikuntha. She is ever at the feet of Bhagavan Vishnu, ever intent on the perennial eternal service of the Lord. This conception of the Goddess Lakshmi is very significant one, that is to be borne in mind and translated into action in the personal life of each model Hindu woman.

Manifestations of Lakshmi in the Home

Coming from the person of the Grihalakshmi to the surroundings of the house, cleanliness is the one important way in which Lakshmi is present. The very dust and dirt about the house is Alakshmi. It is referred to in South India as Daridrya.

Then, lamps. The moment the time of twilight and sunset comes we will immediately find that every Hindu Home will at once have a lamp lit and saluted and thus brightness and illumination will at once come in before darkness sets in. This is a practice which is followed in every Hindu home where it is recognised that light or illumination is an aspect of Lakshmi as She is manifest in the domestic sphere.

Then the worship of the gods. This is of paramount importance. Where the gods are not worshipped, there Lakshmi does not stay. She may of course come and take Her abode in Her extreme

Avidya aspect; money may be accumulated, but ultimately prosperity will go from the home, and grief, suffering and sorrow will be the ultimate fate of those homes where the gods are not worshipped. This is a very important factor which people of this sacred land, who have come to be increasingly influenced by occidental thought and Western ways of living, will have to bear in mind and to beware of if they really wish their ultimate happiness and the prosperity of the family. Gods have to be worshipped; that is to be the most important part of domestic life and observance of the traditional forms of festivity and sacred days. For if these days like the Janmashtami, Rama-Navami, etc., which are observed in this holy land, are neglected, we remark that there is no auspiciousness in that house.

Charity. This is also an important manifestation of Mother Lakshmi in the Grihasthasrama. The Grihastha has the unique privilege of sharing what he has with others of the three Ashramas—the indigent Brahmacharis who wish to carry on their studies, the wandering Sannyasin and also the Vanaprasthin who has renounced home and is living a holy life and preparing to qualify himself for the fourth order of Sannyasa. To give charity to these three classes of beings is a rare privilege of the second Order and to utilise this privilege is to manifest the power of Goddess Lakshmi in the domestic sphere; for, it is by this that preservative aspect of Vishnu is exercised, by which Dharma is preserved and the other Ashramas are helped to be perpetuated.

Hospitality to the Atithi (guest) is an important

aspect of Lakshmi. Where a stranger or a guest is turned away, there Lakshmi does not abide. But where there is a welcome for the beggar, and the unexpected guest, there Lakshmi dwells in all Her radiance and blesses that home. Hospitality, charity and generosity are also important aspects of Goddess Lakshmi which have to be diligently and religiously preserved by the devout Hindu Grihastha.

Two things which are peculiarly Indian, and I may say peculiarly Hindu, which are also important factors in which the Goddess Lakshmi manifests Herself in the Hindu home are these. First, as the sacred basil (Tulsi) plant. No home should ever be without the Tulsi plant. For this is one of the living forms in which the Goddess Lakshmi is present upon earth. She is the direct Vibhuti of the Divine Lord. In this respect I may say that the Maharashtrians are very particular about this; no matter where they might live, they may be millionaires and they may be living in materialistic surroundings in big cities; they may be living in tenements where hundreds of families live together in four or five-storeyed houses; yet you will find that every Maharashtrian home will have a small pot where the Tulsi plant will grow. The moment you enter the house, you will see the Tulsi plant. It is thus that the Mother blesses such families where She is worshipped in this very special form. No Maharashtrian Griha-lakshmi will ever take anything until she has at least offered a flower at this Tulsi plant or burnt a little camphor or done one Pradakshina and bowed her head in devout salutation to Tulsi-Devi.

The second form of the Goddess which is unfortunately fast disappearing from all Hindu homes in the urban areas is the sacred cow—Gomata. It was the custom of all Hindus a couple of generations ago to have the worship of cow every day in the house. Without Gopuja the devout Hindu wife will not take her food. In cities it is very rare to see a cow and all milk is supplied in bottles from dairies. Therefore, this is a tradition that is dying away except in villages. To make up for this even though it may not be possible for the Hindu Grihalakshmi to preserve this tradition, of daily Gopuja, as a sort of Prayaschittha, at least upon one or two sacred days a year every devout Hindu lady must make it a point to perform this Puja. There is of course one particular day in the year which is specially set apart for Gopuja; and upon that day people somehow manage to worship the cow wherever they can find it. Thus opportunities for such Puja should be created where there is this manifestation of the Goddess in the form of the sacred animal the Cow which at one time formed the grand conception of wealth according to the Hindu mind. Thus far for the manifestation of the Mother in the sphere of the house.

Spiritual Wealth in the Sadhaka

Now we come to the most important aspect of the Goddess Lakshmi in this world as the Moksha-Dayini. Mainly Mother in Her aspect of Lakshmi is of the Rajo-Guna; because, through Rajas activity is kept up. Life has to be preserved by dynamic processes. Therefore, the Mother is partaking of the Rajo-Guna.

But yet She has within Herself the inner resources of
Pure Sattva because Vishnu partakes of Sattva Guna
and ultimately She has to merge in Her third aspect
as Goddess Saraswati and as we approach the border-
land between the manifestation of Lakshmi and Saraswati, Mother Lakshmi manifests as Mokshalakshmi—that
is the means that helps us to attain deliverance. In this
aspect it is that the Mother manifests in the life of the
Sadhaka. The Sixteenth Chapter of the Gita gives us
some of the main qualities in which the Mother is
manifest; She is manifest as fearlessness, purity of
heart, steadfastness in knowledge and Yoga, alms-
giving, control of the senses, sacrifice, study of the
scriptures, austerity, straightforwardness, harmlessness,
truth, absence of anger, renunciation, peacefulness, absence of crookedness, compassion to beings, uncovetous-
ness, gentleness, modesty, absence of fickleness. Here
two very interesting points may be noted. In Her
aspect as Avidya Maya, Lakshmi is manifest as wealth
and the concomitants of wealth, viz., greed for more
wealth, the sense of acquisition and pride and vanity
as part and parcel of the Abhimana of wealth; and
also She is manifest as fickleness. It is very significant
when the Lord enumerates the Daivi Sampat upon the
spiritual path. He points some of the aspects of the
Mother which are directly in opposition to Her own
manifestation as the Avidya-Maya. That is why in the
second verse of the Sixteenth Chapter, we get both
non-covetousness as also absence of fickleness. These
are the twenty-four Daivi-Sampat which are aspects in

which the Goddess Lakshmi takes Her abode in the
heart of the spiritual aspirant.

Then Sama and Dama are two divine attributes
that are manifest in the heart of the Sadhaka, serenity
as opposed to fickleness, selflessness as opposed to
selfishness which all possessions bring about. Obedience: this is an important aspect in which the
Mother manifets Herself in the heart of the Sadhaka;
for She is obedience personified in relation to Her
Lord Maha-Vishnu. Even as She denotes the very
acme of Pativratya and absolute absorption in the service of Her Lord, She manifests Herself in the heart
of the Sadhaka and the seeker as spontaneous Guru-
Bhakti that is worshipfulness towards the spiritual
preceptor, and its natural concomitant, i.e., whole-
hearted, dedicated, self-sacrificing service of the
spiritual preceptor, Guru-Seva with Ananya-Bhava.

Mother manifests Herself in the Sadhaka's personality as keen observation, alertness and wakefulness. To have these qualities is of paramount
importance upon the path of Yoga. One should not be
lethargic; one should not miss important things from
which he may have to learn invaluable and priceless
lessons; and therefore the quality of keen observation
is a very necessary one for the spiritual Sadhaka for
he has to learn in this school of life where experience
is the method of education and unless one has got this
power of observation by which he learns valuable lessons through these experiences, he will be missing the
most important aspect of Goddess Lakshmi.

Discipline: one must have spiritual discipline. This

is a sign of auspiciousness because it springs out of self-control and firmness of mind, as the preservative aspect; just as Mother as power gives us the necessary quality of firmness and determination of mind. If this has to bear fruit in Sadhana one must have regular, unbroken and continuous Sadhana. Therefore, continuity in one's spiritual Sadhana and regularity in Sadhana are two ways in which the Goddess Lakshmi as Vishnu-Shakti manifests Herself in the heart of the Sadhaka. For, these two qualities sustain the Yoga-Abhyasa of the seeker.

Persistence and Perseverance: These two are important aspects of Daivi Sampat through which Lakshmi is manifest. Then, a feeling of desirelessness and self-sufficiency, contentment or Santosha are also the expressions of Goddess Lakshmi within our hearts.

Even as cleanliness in the domestic sphere, so also Saucha in the life of a Sadhaka is a necessary expression of Goddess Lakshmi—inner as well as outer cleanliness in all aspects of the seeker's life.

Health and cheerfulness—these two aspects are manifestations of the Goddess.

Slight Not the Mother

Having thus summed up the manifestations of the Mother both in the domestic sphere and the sphere of the life of Yoga and Sadhana, we have to bear in mind an important law with regard to the manifestation of this aspect of the divine power of the Mother. Where Lakshmi is worshipped and propitiated there She stays. Where She is neglected there the Mother does not stay. This is to be always borne in mind by all people whether in the domestic sphere or in the Sadhana-life. Knowing this one must be very careful and avoid all slightings of the Mother. When such manifestations of Goddess Lakshmi are present, if we do not make use of them, if we ignore them, then we slight the Goddess. There, we neglect to honour Her as She would have us honour Her. Therefore, if Lakshmi is neglected and if She is slighted, prosperity and happiness, secular as well as spiritual, will depart from that person.

Realising this important law, we must be ever careful to avoid slighting the Mother in any aspect. Therefore, in the Hindu home we have always the belief that one should not get angry when he is sitting down to take his food. One should not speak harsh words at food-time. To refuse food is a very great blunder; for it becomes a direct insult and slighting of the Goddess in Her visible form of sustaining the very life upon earth. One should never slight food or treat it with disrespect. Therefore, in the Hindu family where this important fact is recognised, the Grihalakshmi will never allow specially rice to be thrown about on the floor, for to tread upon this rice is a very great mistake. Anna is Lakshmi. One should never waste or throw away food unnecessarily, because by this throwing away of food, we fail to recognise the worth and importance of this manifestation of the Goddess. We may by all means give food in charity, by all means feed the animals, the cow, the dog, the cat, any hungry creature; but wantonly we should not throw away food. For, if when She comes to us of Her own gracious will, we thus fail to recognise Her worth, then at a time when we need Her we will find that She is absent.

One more important manifestation of Lakshmi in the Sadhaka is memory. *Yaa Devi Sarva Bhuteshu Smriti Rupena Samsthita*. Therefore, the spiritual seeker must always try to cultivate the Mother in this aspect. Mother is the Smriti in all beings, says the Devi Sukta,—Smriti of the precious and sublime words of Upadesh, of wisdom, of Jnana, from the lips of the Guru, and also from the lips and from the example of all great saints, the men of God in this world from whom we obtain this knowledge. It is through Smriti that these gems of spiritual instructions are preserved; if we do not bear them in mind, reflect over them, do *Manana* and *Nididhyasana* we will not be able to reap the full benefit out of this Upadesha. Unless we have this memory aspect of the Divine Mother in us, we shall never be able to carry out the instructions and orders of the Guru in a satisfactory manner. Therefore we should not neglect this important aspect of the Goddess Lakshmi; and give the excuse "I did not remember." If we do not remember the Guru's Upadesh we will be the losers.

Therefore, may we pray to the Mother Lakshmi to bless us and grace both our homes and our hearts in all these divine aspects of Her Vidya nature and may we make the fullest use of Her presence in our homes and hearts and thus try devoutly to honour and worship the Mother. May we thus attain our eternal welfare here as well as hereafter.

A few special words to all devotees and aspirants who have this unique privilege in this life of having come into the sacred shelter at the feet of our divine Gurudev and have got the unique privilege of trying to mould our lives in accordance with his Upadesh as also to observe the lofty divine life as lived in this sacred and holy place, Ananda Kutir. Herein we have one of the rarest manifestations of Mother Lakshmi in all Her radiance and all Her glory. For She has given Herself to us in the form of this unique Ashram, the unique Institution where all the Daivi Sampats are there in profusion and in divine abundance. For, here is a unique, most auspicious and blessed place where having come into this rare human birth and having had the unique good fortune of Mumukshutva and the crown of the third blessing of contact with a sage established in the highest transcendental realisation of the Atman, we have in addition, been given the blessing of this wonderful place wherein every aspect of our Sadhana is being preserved from day to day and helped in every way.

For the Bhakta there is abundant opportunity to do Upasana in the temple, chant the Name of the Lord and sing Kirtan in the Bhajan Hall and every type of facility to have Sravana, Smarana, and other nine modes of Bhakti, and all facilities for doing Japa in the ideal surroundings in the temple or in the forest, on the unique sacred banks of the Ganga.

For the Vedantin every facility is here to hear

sublime discourses on the Upanishads, to have Satsanga with great souls like Sri Swami Krishnanandaji, and also to have the opportunity of deep meditation in the seclusion of the forest-surroundings.

So, too, for the Karma Yogi. For the Karma Yogi it is a paradise; if only he has got the real wish to spiritualise, to transform his life itself into Sadhana.

So, too, for the Raja Yogi: to develop all the virtues, to practise Asanas and Pranayama—there are the best facilities here.

In short this is what a Sanskrit Pundit might say: a place the like of which *Na Bhuto Na Bhavishyati.*

One very rarely comes across such a wonderful place having every facility for every type of Sadhana through which one could reach the highest goal, the destination of human life, and become eternally blessed. This place is the visible manifestation which the Goddess Lakshmi has bestowed Herself upon unstintedly, in this most glorious and most gracious manner. There is this Ganga, Himalayas, Guru, Govinda-Aradhana and all that is left to us is only to honour and adore this wondrous manifestation of Mother Lakshmi in our lives, by making the best use of this opportunity, by utilising this unique privilege and opportunity which the Lord has bestowed upon us.

As I drew your attention just a while ago, let us not commit the blunder of neglecting all these wonderful divine blessings which the Mother has bestowed upon us in this form; for if we neglect, this rare opportunity will pass away. Life is very uncertain and time is fleeting and this rare unique opportunity of a human birth in such ideal conditions will pass away all too soon. If this is neglected and it becomes too late the regret will be entirely ours and then we shall not be in a position to make up for what we thus lose. Mother, once She has given an opportunity and She has been rejected, will not easily come, and very difficult indeed it will be for us to get such an opportunity once again. Therefore, while the Grace is flowing, in all its abundance, may we be alert and vigilant and fill ourselves with it by all means by being diligent in Sadhana, persisting and persevering in our spiritual practices and thus with the blessings of the Divine Feet of Gurudev and the Grace of Mother Lakshmi let us quickly finish this journey of this life on earth and reach the abode of perennial light, eternal bliss, immortality and divine perfection.

विद्याः समस्तास्तव देवि भेदाः
स्त्रियः समस्ताः सकला जगत्सु ।
त्वयैकया पूरितमम्बयैतत्
का ते स्तुतिः स्तव्यपरापरोक्तिः ॥

ॐ ऐं सरस्वत्यै नमः

CREATION: THE MUSIC OF MOTHER'S VEENA

या कुन्देन्दुतुषारहारधवला या शुभ्रवस्त्रावृता
या वीणावरदण्डमण्डितकरा या श्वेतपद्मासना ।
या ब्रह्माच्युतशंकरप्रभृतिभिर्देवैः सदा वन्दिता
सा मां पातु सरस्वती भगवती निःशेषजाड्यापहा ॥

SALUTATIONS and adorations to the Blessed Divine Mother, the source, sustenance and the ultimate goal of all creation. Salutations again and again to the Blessed Mother in Her knowledge-giving aspect, the originator of the entire phenomenon as well as the culmination and conclusion of all knowledge and of all creative processes. May Her grace be upon us all.

Today we come with our adoring hearts to the Supreme Power of the Almighty in Her aspect as Maha Saraswati, the first manifestation of the pure transcendent being, in the form of the Shabda Brahman. Maha Saraswati is at once the origin and the conclusion of the entire evolutionary process of the Jiva and all phenomena. As the Brahma-Shakti, She is

the Great Power that presides over the commencement of creativity. She presides over the commencement of all manifestation and all projection of names
and forms from the Supreme Tattva, viz., nameless,
formless, beyond the reach of the mind and the senses.
And as such, She is the origin of the entire life-
process, but then, as this life-process flows forth from
the Akhanda Ekarasa Satchidananda and progressively
involves down into greater and greater grossness of
matter, becoming the countless millions of Namarupa
and appearing in the realm of Maha Maya, as the illusory world-play, She recedes into the back-ground
and allows the task of this progression to be carried
on by Her other aspects as Vishnu Maya and the
Divine Durga. But then, when the grace of the
Supreme starts the return of the Jiva and commences
the completing process of this evolutionary circle and
the Jiva once again commences the ascent upon the
inward path of Yoga, shedding and casting back the
different layers of its grosser consciousness and ascending into higher and higher stages of purity, Sattva,
Daivi-Sampat and spirituality once again at the very
pinnacle of his ascent in Yoga, Mother manifests Herself to the Jiva as Maha Saraswati, the Light of pure
Knowledge and manifesting within his consciousness as
the Knowledge of Atma—Atma Jnana or Brahma
Jnana, She completes the circle of evolution and once
again the Jiva is merged in the Para Brahman. Thus,
as creativity, Mother Saraswati is at the origin of this
process of involution from the nameless and formless
Para Brahman, from the One into the many as the ul-

timate Jnana-Dayini as the ultimate manifestation in the form of pure Knowledge. She completes the circle. Thus we have in Her the completion of this entire world-play, and in both of these aspects the Mother is worshipped, and to the seeker—to the Sadhaka and to the Yogi—especially, the Mother is particularly significant and important as the bestower of Supreme Wisdom and Jnana by which he attains Kaivalya Moksha.

Theory and Practice of Yoga

The form of the Mother, we find, expresses this supreme dual function of Mother Saraswati. She has in Her hand the Veena, the meaning of which we shall consider presently, but in Her other hands we find the Mother having the spotless *Sphatika Mala* and the Veda Grantha. She has the Book. Pustaka and Mala are the two things She holds, and these signify for us the fact that Mother holds in Herself the entire knowledge of the Apara as well as the Para Tattva. The entire Vedas, as they embody the fullest knowledge of all created things as also the fullest knowledge of the Ultimate Source and Origin of all creation, i.e., Para Brahman,—this She holds in Her hand for She is the dynamic counterpart of Brahma from whom the Vedas have first emanated. Brahma is the Veda-Pita and the Veda-Data. The Mother as Saraswati, is but the Shakti of Brahma, the Chaturmukha Brahma, and therefore She is the expression of the Vedic knowledge which Brahma represents, of which He is the supreme original repository, and as such She bears in Her hand the book of the Vedas, embodying the theory of Brahma-Jnana. In the path of Realisation, the actual Abhyasa of this Vedic knowledge of the truths thus got from the Vedas directly from the books as also from the lips of the Guru,—the theory of this knowledge thus obtained has to be made, converted, into Anubhava through Abhyasa and Nididhyasana and this practical Abhyasa of Vedic truth in the form of Yoga Sadhana is represented by the pure *Sphatika Mala* in the right hand of the Mother. The significance of the Mala is to be equated to Yoga Abhyasa in its practical form. So She embodies the power as it is in thoretical form of the Vedic knowledge and also the dynamic power as it is expressed in and through the practical process of Yoga and spiritual Sadhana.

Mother Is Absolute Purity

Mother is represented as being spotlessly clad in the purest white raiment and also She is Herself the spotless and unblemished and fairest of the fairest beings. Her fairness is likened unto the spotless fairness of the lily, and of the Moon as also the eternal virgin snow-chains represented by the Himalayas. *Ya kundendu tusharahara dhavala. Kunda* means lily; *indu* is Moon. *Tusharahara* means snow-chain. She is white as these three superlatively spotless and white things we know of in this world. She is clad in the pure white raiment. This is to bring out the fact of the Mother being a mass of absolute Suddha-Sattva, because She is the first original emanation from the Para-Brahman.

Mother Is All

We know that according to the Vedas, the first original emanation from the bosom of the Absolute, the Unmanifest, the Nirakara Nirguna, was in the form of the Pranava. The first *spandan*, the mysterious vibration, that took place with the origination of the pure *satsankalpa*, the first will of the Transcendent Divine, which the Vedas express in the form of *Ekoham bahusyaam prajayeya* "I am one, may I become many." It is symbolically expressed in this form so that we may have some idea as to how the One became the apparent many, and its first Suddha-Sankalpa is manifest as a vibration that becomes immediately expressed as the solemn and the mysterious original sound or Nada, which, we all know, as the Supreme Pranava. This Nada Brahma or Pranava is the very form of Mother. Mother Saraswati is Pranava-Rupini. In Her we find manifest the two aspects of this Shabda-Brahman or the Nada-Brahman. The Shabda is the Pranava; Nada is its original sound-form and when it has been articulated in the form of the actual Pranava, it comes into the region of Vani and, therefore, the Mother is referred to as both Veena Vani. She has got the instrument which produces the pure sound and She is Herself the origin of all articulated Name and in this form She is Vani. This sound of the Veena is the very origin of all Vedic Mantras. We find if we carry out this process to its logical conclusion that the entire world will be known to us as nothing more, and nothing less, than the Music of the Supreme Mother's Veena. The entire Jagat, all crea-

tion, is nothing but the manifest form of the music
that flows forth perennially through the Veena of
Mother Saraswati. For, we know that all the visible
universe is made up of form. Whatever we can see,
touch and observe through our senses is in the shape
of form. Rupa is the ultimate way in which the world
is known to us, and each form in this universe is expressed through a certain name. All the meaning of
the innumerable forms of which this universe is made
up, is embodied in countless names (Namas). These
names are but a combination of certain letters or Aksharas. The Aksharas that go to make up the innumerable, different, names or Namas, are nothing but
the articulate expression of sound. Sound articulated
becomes manifest as Akshara, and these mysterious
Akshara Swarupas when combined go to form Nama,
the meaning of which springs forth in the form of
Rupa. That is the Drishya-Jagat. This Nada or sound
which each one of these letters or Aksharas are articulate expressions of,—this Nada is ultimately in its essence pure vibration, and this vibration is the
movement of the Veena of the Mother.

Thus we see in the Mother's Veena, the celestial
strings of the Saraswati Veena, which spring into vibration and manifest as Nada, which are articulated as
definite Aksharas that go to form names, and these
names are expressed in their outward meaningfulness
in countless forms, which become the Jagat. Therefore, the entire visible world, this entire macrocosm—
not only this, but all the countless infinite worlds that
have flowed forth and keep flowing forth every minute

through the Transcendental Essence—are nothing but
the outward expressions of the music of Mother's
Veena. She is the power behind this music. She is the
Supreme Suddha Sattva, the ultimate Tattva by meaning into which we immediately pass on to a state of
pure transcendence and Absolute Existence. This is
what Mother is to us. Her Veena is, therefore, the
Omkara Rupa and the entire world is therefore the
manifestation of Her Power expressed at the origin
through Her Veena in the form of pure Divine Nada.

The Light Before Which Darkness Vanishes

We find in the 'Saptasati' Mother also is manifest
as one of the forms that confront the Asura,
Mahishasura, when the time for his annihilation
comes. This is a rather curious point which is interesting to understand. When we find that the entire
creativity is the special function of the Mother in Her
aspect as Maha Saraswati, how came it that She also
appears in the field of battle in *roudra* aspect? What
destruction can pure creativity be ever called upon to
do? But this point will at once become clear to us
when we bring to our mind for a moment Mother's
aspect at the other terminal of the evolutionary
process when the circle gets completed viz., in the
form of pure Brahma-Jnana. For She does not actually
destroy, as it were, but the moment one reaches
Her,—the moment She manifests in the glory and bril-
liance of Her Light, there is instantaneous cessation of
the cycle of birth and death. Therefore, by the very
fact of Her mere appearance, immediately the disease
of Samsara is destroyed, death meets its death at the

very manifestation of the glory of Mother and the
darkness of ignorance is annihilated. Therefore She
does not actually have to destroy anything, but by Her
mere appearance Ajnana—darkness, gets destroyed by
itself. Therefore the Samsara Chakra is stopped and
She once for all puts an end to even the last remnant
of Jadatva in the Jeeva. The Jeeva becomes one with
the Suddha Chaitanya Brahman. The mere appearance
and the manifestation of Maha Saraswati in the field
of consciousness is enough immediately to annihilate
all the darkness of ignorance, to end all Jadatva, and
destroy death itself and annihilate the entire process
of *"Punarapi jananam punarapi maranam"*, and thus
Mother by Her mere appearance bestows on the Jeeva
the fullness of Brahma Jnana. Thus we find that our
worship of the Mother has a very beautiful significance, in that it not only is the adoration of that
Supreme Power which is to work out our ultimate
release, but it is also at one and the same time the
adoration of the Virat, for when we adore the Mother
as Maha Saraswati, we adore the entire universe, for
we have learned just now that the entire universe is
nothing but a direct expression and manifestation of
Her Power expressed in the first instance as the
Supreme Divine Sound. Therefore, whatever we see is
but the power of Mother Saraswati become crystallised
in form. While we offer our adorations to Mother, we
will not only be offering adorations to the Great
Supreme Being in Its Motherhood aspect, but we shall
be adoring at once the universal form of the Lord
Himself. At the same time, we shall be propitiating

that aspect of the Supreme Power by whose grace alone we shall be ultimatelly released from the clutches of darkness of ignorance, and we shall be taken to the Transcendent Abode of Immortality, Infinite Knowledge and Perennial Bliss.

चितिरूपेण या कृत्स्नमेतद्व्याप्य स्थिता जगत् ।
नमस्तस्यै नमस्तस्यै नमस्तस्यै नमो नमः ॥

ॐ प्रणो देवी सरस्वती वाजेभिर्वाजिनीवती । धीनामवित्र्यवतु ॥

THE GODDESS OF SUCCESS

जय सरस्वति जय सरस्वति जय सरस्वति पाहि माम् ।
श्री सरस्वति श्री सरस्वति श्री सरस्वति रक्ष माम् ॥

SALUTATIONS to the Supreme Divine Mother, who is the substratum and the ultimate goal of all this universe. Salutations to the Mother, the Brahma Rupini, who is the mysterious indescribable power of the Transcendent Reality. Our adorations again and again to Her, the Supreme Shakti, the Adi Shakti, the Para Shakti, who manifests as Saraswati, grants us all release from this phenomenal existence of pain and death by conferring upon us the Supreme Knowledge of Para Brahman.

The entire visible creation, all phenomena, Anantakoti Brahmandas, beyond human ken are all the wondrous and glorious manifestations of Mother Saraswati. She is the Primal Power aspect of the Supreme Being, who is beyond all comprehension, and it is She that first manifests Herself as the mysterious Nada, and is, therefore, worshipped as Nadarupini Saraswati. She is Chidrupini or Shabdarupini also, be-

cause She is the very embodiment of the Supreme
Pranava. The Transcendental Existence is pure Consciousness. It is motionless, actionless, Nishkriya. There
is not the least movement or vibration. It is Nishpanda
and there arises no sound, no action, no movement in
it. It is Ashabda, Nishpanda, Nishkriya. In this infinite
mass of consciousness, Ananda Ghana, the Vedas
declare how there first manifests one point of primal
stress. This point of stress in the mass of consciousness
is the mysterious Bindu, the origin of all things that
are and the Bindu expresses itself as the Nada. The
Adi-spanda manifesting as the point of stress in the
mass of infinite consciousness expresses itself as Nada,
and this is the great Mother Saraswati. And therefore
it is, as we saw, that the Mother is conceived of as the
pure, spotless Being clad in white, where there is no
variation of any colour and bearing the Veena which
embodies, as it were, the force of all Nada. From
Nada, which is the primal sound, in the form of pure
Dhvani, gradually the entire manifestation starts as articulate sound. The articulate sound is Vak, and Vak
is expressed as the Varna or the letter, and combinations of letter-sounds go to form the word or the
Nama, and the Artha of this Nama, the meaning embodied in the name becomes expressed as the form.
Whatever we see in this phenomenal universe is of the
nature of formfulness. This phenomenon, which is
Ananta-rupa is ultimately in the nature of infinite effects of the Primal Shabda Brahman, or Mother Saraswati, having gradually progressed through these
various phases as Dhvani, Vak, Varna, Nama and then

Rupa. And this Transcendental Essence of all manifested creation is also specially manifest in this world of men and things. This is what we shall see today. For, when we had the occasion during the previous days of adoring the Mother in Her aspects as Durga, the powerful, the dissolver of Namarupa, and as Lakshmi, the preserver, protector and sustainer of all Namarupa in Trikala, we referred to Them not only in Their original cosmic aspects but also in their manifest aspects upon this plane of man and his activities in this Vyavaharic world, and also as they were inwardly manifest in the consciousness and in the personality of the seeker, Jiva, progressing upon the inner path of Yoga Sadhana towards the goal of perfection and reunion with the Supreme Soul called Para Brahman. Even so when we come to consider the Mother as She may be manifest in this world of men and things we find that the Goddess Saraswati though manifest upon this external world of Vyavahara and the various activities of man, yet She is not quite so much manifest as the Supreme Para Shakti as Durga and Lakshmi, and there is a reason for this, for the Mother is, as it were, at the two terminals of the cyclic process of involution and evolution back down to the Primal Source. We have seen how Mother is the creative impulse. She is the one who presides over the coming into manifestation of the unmanifest Transcendent, and as such in the world Her function is primary and then She withdraws into the background. Once things have come into manifestation and the Nameless has taken Namarupa, then She recedes, handing over the further processes to Her other aspects manifest through the Goddess Lakshmi and the Goddess Durga. Therefore it is that we are more aware—our notice is more drawn towards the play of Shakti in Its preservative aspect; for this is spread over the field of time, for we find this is a continuous process. Therefore naturally the attention of man is more fixed upon this aspect and also upon the final play of the Mother as the dispassionate dissolver of all names and forms. And there is this very natural and understandable reason for this state of affairs, i.e., for the other two aspects being more in the attention and consciousness of man, and the reason is that due to the *Mamata* or 'mineness' and the intense attachment born out of mineness that man has towards Namarupa, towards the objects of this universe, he is specially interested in their sustenance, in their continuing in existence, and his attention is especially shocked and is arrested by their going out of existence. His intense attachment due to mineness does not like the idea of its dissolution. He is grieved and his attraction, therefore, brings the process of dissolution to loom very large in his mind. He is always aware of it and fears it and therefore it occupies his mind. He actively participates in this function of Mother as Lakshmi, in preserving things which he feels to be 'mine'. But, the creativity of thing which spontaneously springs from Mother Saraswati, once it is done, it is taken for granted and it does not occupy the positive attention of man, and therefore, the presence of the Mother as Saraswati-Tattva is not so much recognised. But it stands to reason that She is indispensably there. Because, but for creation, things will not exist to get attached to. From the very nature of things the Mother who is taken for granted is an indispensable factor for everything which has come into being.

The Secret of Success

She is not only the outflow of the process of creativity, She is also all commencement, because commencement is that point from which creativity starts; and therefore in Hindu society the Mother is worshipped as all Arambha. Everything that starts is attributed to the grace of Goddess Saraswati. It is a very peculiar factor that side by side with Mother as Saraswati, presiding over all Arambha or beginning, the devout Hindu also worships the special aspect of the Deity as Ganapathy. But here Ganapathy too is an aspect—but a negative one—of Arambha. For, He also represents Wisdom, but Mother represents creative aspect of wisdom and the special worship of Ganapathy, which is more known than the worship of Saraswati, is done more with the intention of warding off obstacles, whereas the positive aspect of worship that She may bestow by Her grace success on all things started is always centralised upon the adoration of Mother Saraswati. Let us consider how in this aspect Mother is manifest in this visible universe of man. Day after tomorrow for instance, we will see a special occasion when Mother is invoked and adored as the Deity presiding over all commencement. For, it has come down through holy tradition that Vijaya-Dasami is set apart for Vidyarambha—commencement of studies whether science or arts, on this day of Vijaya-Dasami is considered extremely auspicious and conducive to fruition. All musical instruments, and everything connected with creative art, all things connected with these creative processes in the communal life of man, is the object of adoration and worship on this Vijaya Dasami Day, and we find that the manifest form of the word, of the letter, as embodied in books, is decorated and it is worshipped in the traditional form, and after adoring Mother on the 9th, on the 10th day at a proper Muhurtha these books are taken out and the Vidyarambha commences.

This is upon the plane of the external activities of man; side by side we will find, and especially in this Ashram, that the inward commencement of spiritual life also is signified on this day by the spiritual aspect of this Arambha in the form of Upadesha. As you know, the mystic sound takes the form of Vak, Varna. All Mantras are mysterious occult combinations of these Varnas. A Mantra is a mass of localised Saraswati-Sakti and the Japa of the Mantra bestows transcendental knowledge upon the Sadhaka. This aspect of Saraswati is given to all seekers in the form of Mantra Upadesha. This is also the starting point of the inner spiritual evolution in the Sadhaka. The pure Spatika Mala which She holds stands for the practice of the Vedic knowledge which She holds in the form of the Pustaka in the other hand.

In the wider life of mankind in this world, when we view it through his understanding of the play of the Para Sakti in Her aspect as Saraswati, we will find that whatever creative activity goes on in this world is ultimately an attribute of Mother Saraswati. Therefore, the scientific researches carried on both here and in the super-scientific Occident, and discoveries that result from these scientific researches and the inventions which they make out of the discoveries of scientific laws and all the applications of such inventions are therefore the play of Divine Mother Saraswati. Scientific researches, discoveries, inventions and the manufacture of various appliances based on such inventions—these are the direct manifestations of Mother Saraswati.

We have also said that side by side, Mother is there as commencement, and therefore, She is the supreme spiritual point of commencement of the day; that is, when the four Praharas of the night are ended and night recedes and a fresh new day commences in the solemn moment of the sacred Brahma-Muhurtha. There you have the fullest manifestation of Saraswati. It is permeated by the spiritualising power of Jnanadayini Saraswati. The new year also for this self-same reason is an auspicious moment pervaded with the Spiritual Power of the Divine Sakti in Her aspect as Saraswati. The commencement of any new business, for instance, should be done with the devout adoration of Mother Saraswati. For then, She will out of Her grace bestow success on the new enterprise. It is only Her play that makes possible the founding of any new institution or commencement of any new enterprise. This is also a manifestation of Mother Saraswati, and it is a very common sight particularly here, at Ananda

Kutir, that any commencement is first of all solemnised by invoking the blessings of Mother Saraswati. Also the commencement of every new phase, during the process of the construction for instance, the digging of the foundation-laying of the corner-stone, is preceded by the worship of Mother Saraswati.

Similarly, all trades and all activities are to be done in a spirit of devout worshipfulness and in a spirit of Puja of the Mother as Saraswati, and to a great extent this practice is followed, at least to my knowledge, in almost all the business houses in South India. I have noted it is the other aspect of the resultant money that is more remembered and regarded in the Maharashtra state, where business people are more the votaries of Lakshmi, the Goddess of Wealth, rather than of Saraswati. But either way, the worship goes to the Supreme Deity. But we must realise that all these movements in human activity are but the play of Para Shakti in Her various forms, be it Lakshmi, Durga or Saraswati. Realising this, we must approach all activity and we must engage in all activity in a devout spirit, in a solemn and devout Bhava, of pure Puja of Parashakti and thus alone we shall be able to utilise even the activities of Vyavahara for the evolution of our spiritual life. If this is done, we shall find that we shall not have much room to complain about the lack of opportunity and the absence of enough time for the man of the world to engage in worship, meditation and Yoga Sadhana, because it is a failure to recognise the spiritual nature of all activities and to perceive the Hand of Mother in all activities.

It is this that makes man to think that he cannot do Spiritual Sadhana and there are no hopes of his Spiritual Illumination. This is a sad mistake, for the devout Hindu and the Indian genius conceives all life as a means to the Supreme end of Self-realisation. To the devout Hindu, life has no greater meaning than that of an opportunity afforded to the Jiva to quickly finish his evolution and reach the goal of human life, viz., Self-realisation. Therefore we must try to live as such, for there is nothing secular to the Hindu, and to him all movements are the manifestations of the Divine Mother and activities are a continuous worship of Para Shakti, and realising this, we must change our entire attitude towards activity. We should not feel that we are fallen, or we are far from the spiritual Reality, in our secular activities, and spend the life regretting for the lack of opportunity for Sadhana. On the other hand, all work should be done in a spirit of joy, in a spirit of enthusiasm, and in an elevated state of mind, for one must know all is Matri Puja. Therefore one should do it in a spirit of inspired worshipfulness and we will find that there is no need for man either to change his profession or place or to run away to a forest and try to live an exclusive life of the conventional mode of Nivritti. If the time comes for a life of seclusion and meditation, well and good, but if this is not possible, as is the case with the vast majority, there need be no regret, for, indirectly, everything is Yoga, and everything is spiritual Sadhana, once the correct attitude is adopted and the proper view of things is accepted. This is the special truth which we may find revealed through the nine days' adoration of the Divine Mother. If the hand works, eyes see, nose smells, ears hear and tongue utters—all these movements are the worship of the Mother in Her Dynamic aspect. And to remind us of this, our wise ancients have given us this rare blessing, privilege of the Navaratra Puja of the Blessed Divine Mother. Therefore it is the primary duty of all mankind, the children of the Divine Mother, not to forget this great privilege conferred upon them of continually worshipping the Mother in and through all life's activities.

Let us rejoice in having this gift of human birth and in having this gift of capacity to act and move for the glorification of the Mother. We have in our hand a rare opportunity for attaining the highest goal of Self-realisation and if we make use of this outer form of Mother's Worship in the form of spiritualised activity, later on we shall be graced by the Mother; She will bestow upon us the inner form of this worship in the form of contact with sages and in the form of their grace, Upadesha and Diksha. She will come in the form of Mantra, and as we progress, She will manifest Herself as the supreme Dhyana, which is the gateway to illumination and ultimately She will illumine our consciousness as Samadhi, for Her ultimate manifestation in the individual is as Samadhi and Self-Knowledge. When thus She manifests Herself, the goal of life is achieved, our life's work is done, our worship of Mother is complete and then we shall have no more to do but to enjoy the Supreme Perennial Bliss of the Para-Brahman, this mysterious Shakti that the Mother is.

सवित्रीभिर्वाचां शशिमणिशिलाभङ्गरुचिभि-
र्वशिन्याद्याभिस्त्वां सह जननि संचिन्तयति यः ।

स कर्ता काव्यानां भवति महतां भङ्गिरुचिभि-
र्वचोभिर्वाग्देवीवदनकमलामोदमधुरैः ॥

O Mother! Who meditates on you together with Vashini and others who bestow eloquence and who are like the fissure of moon-stone (Sasimani) in lustre, he becomes the author of great literary master-pieces, which are charming in their expressions and whose words are sweet due to the fragrance of the lotus of Saraswati's mouth.

ॐ भूर्भुवस्वः तत्सवितुर्वरेण्यं भर्गो देवस्य धीमहि धियो यो
नः प्रचोदयात्

NINTH NIGHT

THE PATH TO FINAL LIBERATION

गीता गंगा च गायत्री गोविन्देति हृदि स्थिते ।
चतुर्गकारसंयुक्ते पुनर्जन्म न विद्यते ॥

SALUTATIONS to Her through Whose Grace
alone the Knowledge of the Ultimate Reality dawns
upon the consciousness of earnest seekers. Salutations
to the great Mother who keeps up this mysterious
divine Drama of creation, preservation and destruction. Salutations to Her Who makes the transcendent,
unmanifest essence, to be manifest as infinite names
and forms, through Her mysterious Power, and Who
deludes and binds the Jivas to this world-process.
Salutations to Her again as the Supreme Vidya-Maya
Who in Her aspect as Maha Saraswati brings about ultimate deliverance from the bondage of nescience and
phenomenal existence and bestows upon the seeker,
the highest transcendent beatitude or Supreme State
of Kaivalya.

Today is the last day, the ninth of the nine-day
worship of the Mother. It is through Her supreme

compassion and grace that we have been given this precious opportunity and occasion for expressing our devotion and adoration of Her Divine Feet, by doing which we elevate our minds and our consciousness and take one more step forward towards the ultimate goal of Atma-Sakshatkara.

Her grace is infinite. Her compassion and love for all human beings and especially the seekers and aspirants is simply indescribable. The mother is ever eager to take the child into her arms. Even so the Divine Mother who has set going this momentary play, this divine Drama upon this stage of the external physical universe is yet in the core of our heart and is at the same time eager to take back into Her Infinite Bosom those children who have had enough of this play and who have lost interest in the play and stopping short, they turn back and cry 'Mother.' "Mother! No more of this play for me. Long have I wandered away from Thee. Therefore, bestow Thy Grace upon me. Take this child back into Thy blissful arms." This is the cry of the Jiva. This is the Mumukshutva. This is the aspiration. This is the call of the infinite to the finite. When the finite individual hears this call, ceases to be interested in this world-play and turning his back upon it as it were he begins to gaze into the face of the Mother, then it is that the compassion-filled eyes of the great Mother open for a while and the rays of Her divine mercy fall upon and bathe this child and once for all the fatigue, the strain and the dust of this play, drop away from him; and he is lifted up into the subtle heights of spiritual bliss.

Then the child regains the Mother's arms and for him the stress and the struggle of the play is over and there is but Pure Bliss, the bliss of having regained his coveted home. For, we are all wanderers, children who have strayed away from our original home, the Supreme Abode of Satchidananda. To realise that we have strayed far away and long enough and to once again desire keenly to regain that original home of Satchidananda is the entire meaning and the process of the spiritual quest. This is spiritual life and this is Sadhana Marga.

As we know, the great Mother is both Vidya-Maya as also Avidya-Maya. In both these aspects, She has Her play upon this world-stage in Her threefold forms of Durga, Lakshmi and Saraswati. Yesterday we saw how Mother in Her Supreme Sattvic aspect as Saraswati, the Omkara-Rupini, the Nada-Svarupini, was manifest upon the external field of human activity in Her Pravritti aspect. Mother, though She is Supreme Vidya, yet She has in Her a tinge of the mysterious Avidya-Maya also and in this aspect of the Avidya Maya She is manifest as the Saraswati Tattva in Pravritti.

But, predominantly Mother Saraswati is Vidya; and in Her glorious Vidya-Maya aspect, She manifests Herself variously upon the Nivritti, the inward life of the Jiva. It is by a consideration of the Mother in the inward, Nivritti life, that we shall offer our homage and adoration to Her Lotus Feet this day. For Pravritti we have seen She is all creative activity. We have seen how She is all constructive activity. She is at the beginning of all things. She is the research faculty of the scientist. She is the poetic faculty of the votary of the muse. She is the artistic talent of the musician, the painter, the sculptor and all the followers of fine arts. She is the discoveries the scientist makes in his period of keen research. Mother Saraswati again appears as the inventions, whatever they are, that flow out of the keen probings of the intellect into the outward nature. She is again all those various products that result out of these inventions. Mother is also all constructive avocation. She is all the professions, all the trades; She is the business acumen of the super-salesman. She is education upon the external field of man's Pravritti activities. Thus, Mother appears variously in the outside world.

We touched upon a few of Her aspects in the inward, reverse process, the Path of going back from the many into the Supreme Source, the Transcendent One, the Absolute. In the Nivritti path which is the inward life of the aspirant's soul, which is the inward life of the Jiva on the path of Yoga and Sadhana, we saw how She manifests as the Diksha of the Guru. She is also the Mantra and the Japa of the Mantra, the Sadhana with the Mantra like Anushthana, etc. We have seen how Mother Saraswati is a radiant mass of purest Shuddha Sattva, how She is the purest Sattva embodied as it were. These are symbolised by Her spotless white raiment, as also Her own dazzling fairness.

Mother As Supreme Sattva

As Sattva She manifests in the heart of the

spiritual aspirant and as the Grace of Saraswati dawns upon the aspirant, his entire life undergoes a transformation. All the grossness and bestiality that is in him is slowly and gradually, but surely, cast aside. For, in the radiant whiteness of Sattva, the darkness of Tamas cannot stand. Sattva is a superior, positive force in the life of the being. Therefore, with the advent of Sattva as manifest by Mother Saraswati's Grace, Tamo-Guna decreases and ultimately it is completely overcome by the aspirant. The extremely gross lower appetites which once were the most pleasure-giving things to him which he revelled and indulged in, begin to become painful to the aspirant; he abhors them. Grossness is something which becomes foreign to one in whom Saraswati has come to dwell.

Even so, there happens a change in the Rajo-Guna that is there in the individual. Rajas is activity springing out of selfishness. It is activity under the urge of greed, covetousness and selfishness. Activity or dynamism is always good. It is a valuable asset to all beings in every endeavour and attempt towards any attainment. But when it is engendered by selfishness, greed or covetousness, when it is directed by these baser elements in being, then Rajas takes the man outward and enmeshes him in greater and greater bondage; but when the higher pull of a greater power, the power of Sattva begins to manifest and to work within the aspirant in his Nivritti life, then surely, its effect and influence are felt upon the Rajo-Guna in him; and this Rajas rather than being subservient to selfishness and greed begins to be controlled, diverted and canalised into higher and more sublime channel. The Rajo-Guna, the dynamic power, which is in him now becomes allied, not to Tamas, but to Sattva. Therefore, it becomes a valuable asset to him upon his spiritual life. It is controlled and sublimated and diverted to higher, nobler, spiritual pursuits. He is active now for the good of others; he is animated by noble Sattvic virtues like compassion, mercy, selflessness, and by the pure desire to offer worship to the visible Lord as manifest in and through all creatures, in the form of Karma Yoga or Seva. Thus both the Lower natures of Tamas and of Rajas are removed from the spiritual path as obstacles. Tamo-Guna ceases to be; it only lurks in him in its other manifestations like the daily sleep, etc; but in its grosser form it ceases to be. The Rajo-Guna also begins to be a friend and helper to the aspirant, through the Grace of Mother Saraswati when She manifests in his Nivritti life in Her aspect as Pure Sattva-Guna.

If you read the Seventeenth Chapter of the Bhagavad Gita where the classification of all qualities and things into these three categories of Sattva, Rajas and Tamas is given, we may conclude that in this Gunatraya-Vibhaga, Mother Saraswati is that which is declared to be Sattvic. In the spiritual life of the Sadhaka and the seeker-disciple, Mother is the Yoga and Sadhana and ultimately She is the unfoldment of the consciousness into the radiance of Jnana. As Sattva in the individual activity of the Sadhaka, She manifests Herself as Sadachara. Sadachara as we know is the very basis of success in the entire spiritual life. It forms the foundation. The Yama-Niyama of Raja Yoga are the most scientific expressions of Sadachara.

Guru's Word Is Gospel Truth

As the Vak or the Supreme Sound or the Word, Mother is manifest to the aspirant first as the Guru Mantra which the aspirant receives through Diksha; and if we are to worship with due honour Mother as the Mantra, then it behoves every spiritual aspirant to diligently practise this Divine Name which he has received from the Sat-Guru. Neglect of the Mantra, neglect to practise this Divine Name received from the Guru will be indeed a failure to worship and to give the due honour to Mother Saraswati. If we thus neglect Her, our spiritual progress will be retarded.

In a more general aspect, She is manifest to the aspirant upon the Path of Yoga and in spiritual life as the instructions and the day-to-day Upadesha of the Guru. Thus the aspirant must have the proper attitude of worshipfulness and he must receive the instructions of the Guru in a very solemn and in a very serious spirit. He should not be heedless. He should not have a very casual attitude towards the words of the Guru. To the aspirant the words of the Guru must be gospel-truth. For they are as Mantra to him: *Mantra-mulam Gurorvakyam.* This lapse of taking the ordinary words of the Guru in a very light manner or too casually and failing to pay proper heed to the words of the Guru, are very widely prevalent errors in the aspirant-world. For all Sadhakas and disciples it so happens that close contact with the Sat-Guru often makes them to be less

receptive to the Saraswati manifest through Him as
Upadesha and Vak; and by this heedlessness, they
stand to lose much. Therefore, we must be very
cautious in our attitude towards the Guru's words, to
this aspect of the Mother, that they represent. If only
we take them in the right spirit and receptivity and
carry them out diligently, then the Grace of Mother
Saraswati would be utilised properly and profitably.

Svadhyaya: Its Practical Value

In addition to these, She is also manifest in two
special aspects of spiritual Sadhana. We have said that
Mother Saraswati is actually an embodiment of the
Vedas. Vedas mean transcendent knowledge of the
Supreme Being. Upanishads are the highest reaches of
the Vedas. We have been told how the very quint-
essence of these Upanishads was given to humanity in
the form of the Bhagavad Gita. Therefore, Mother is
present to the aspirant in the form of this unique
universal scripture, Srimad Bhagavad Gita. Therefore,
all great spiritual teachers, Acharyas, have enjoined
upon the seekers to regularly, daily, study the Gita.
We must always worship the Mother in Her form as
the Gita, by unfailingly going to the Gita every day
and trying to imbibe the gospel of the Gita gradually
into our own lives. This instruction to read the Gita
has been specially stressed in the Dinacharya which
Gurudev has given to all aspirants living the divine
life at his sacred feet. We also know that in the
Niyama of the Patanjali Darshana, Svadhyaya is one of
the important items.

We have seen how Mother Saraswati the Parashabda or the Primal Sound is manifest in Her various progressive aspects as Dhvani, then the articulate sound or Vak, and the specific Vak in the form of letters of the alphabet, and combination of letters giving us the Nama or the name and the Artha of the Nama appearing before us in the form of Rupa. As Mother is thus embodied in and through the sacred letters of the scriptures, all spiritual books and also Dharma-Granthas and all scriptures are therefore a mass of Saraswati Tattva. She gives us the knowledge of the Transcendent Being in and through Her Form as the written letter and the word. Therefore, when we take up the spiritual scripture and study it as part of our daily routine, we actually come into contact of Saraswati and try to be instructed by Her direct as She is manifest in the word.

Svadhyaya is an important Anga of daily Sadhana. Its importance to the spiritual aspirant is manifold; but at least one very significant part which Svadhyaya plays in the realm of Sadhana may just be touched upon, for it will show us how it helps to increase the Sattva and spiritual qualities in the thoughts, in the Bhava or consciousness of the seekers. It is in this way. We know the entire nature and the make-up of the spiritual Sadhana is decided by one's Samskaras. The mind is everything; and the mind is but a bundle of Samskaras. These Samskaras are acquired by Vyavahara. Contact with external objects, moving with persons, the experience of these contacts, go to form more and more Samskaras in the being. In this external world of

Vyavahara, specially so in the field of Karma Yoga, we find that Samskaras of a totally Anatmic nature, that are totally inimical to spiritual life and spiritual progress, Samskaras of Vyavahara, of Pravritti, of the Vishayas are gathered together in abundance every day by the human being in his daily round of normal external activities. If these Samskaras go on increasing day by day, they become a terrible downward pull, a force tending to externalise and making the mind more and more Vishayakara. But they cannot be completely avoided. It is impossible to completely cut off all Vyavahara for the vast majority of spiritual seekers. Therefore, as a supreme psychological method of counteracting these Samskaras, these ideas, spiritual ideas are made to get into the mind through daily study of elevating scriptures. For by daily, diligent and regular study of scriptures, every day the spiritual aspirant takes into himself a whole mass of sublime spiritualising, life-transforming ideas; and they form powerful, positive, Sattvic, spiritual Samskaras in the mind of the seeker. Thus, they help to overcome the unfortunate unspiritual Samskaras that are gathered inevitably during the course of daily Vyavahara. They have got the power to give a fresh Bhava to the aspirant. They change the thoughts, the Samskaras and the very Bhava of the aspirant. This daily feeding of the nature of the seeker with spiritual and Sattvic food in the form of ideas is achieved by our contact with Mother Saraswati in Her form of sacred scriptures— the lives of Saints, Gita, Bhagavata, Ramayana, Bible, Quran, Zend Avesta, Dhammapada.

Also, we find this creation of a set of powerful positive spiritual ideas in the mind help the aspirant during Dhyana, during the practice of concentration and inward meditation. We find that when an aspirant tries to do Dhyana, the mind wanders. In the beginning stages of Dhyana, this wandering is very powerful. The entire process becomes a see-saw, a sort of tug of war; the mind is brought to the Lakshya and it wanders again. There is one very undesirable thing here; when it wanders, the field of its idea in which this wandering takes place is all sensual, gross and worldly. This wandering cannot be arrested except by gradual practice and Vairagya. But in the meantime a change can be brought about; even if the mind wanders, provided that a whole set of powerful spiritual ideas are daily pushed into the mind through Svadhyaya, the field of ideas through which the mind wanders in its Vikshepa becomes gradually Sattvic. Instead of wandering in a vicious set of ideas, the mind has now a field of pure ideas, great ideas, elevating, Sattvic ideas through which it wanders. The wandering then becomes less harmful to the aspirant. In this way also the daily Svadyaya is an invaluable asset to the aspirant.

Speak Little

Let us come to the actual conduct, the Achara, of the spiritual aspirant. Here we may give a few hints that will be very valuable for the aspirant in his daily conduct. Mother, we have seen, is speech. She is manifest in all beings as Vak. She is Vakshakti. Therefore, to conserve speech through a regular period of

Mouna is also the adoration of Mother Sarawati. This energy of the Mother in the form of Vak, when conserved, becomes an asset to the aspirant to be tapped and utilised in the Yogic process of Pratyahara, Dharana and Dhyana; and also the conserved power of Vak in and through the Sadhana of Mouna becomes very valuable in carrying out Vichara and self-analysis. This is practical experience which any aspirant may see for himself, by practising Mouna. As long as the Vak is spent outward, the mind becomes outgoing,—one cannot do the same intense Vichara and introspection. But when the Vakshakti is conserved through Mouna it becomes capable of being utilised for inwardness, for introspection and the practice of Viveka and Vichara.

Speak the Truth

It is the great duty of spiritual aspirants to safeguard the sanctity of this holy power of Vak. We have to safeguard the sanctity of the power of Mother Saraswati in the form of Vak. We know that falsehood is unspiritual, unclean. Therefore, the aspirant who would aspire to realise the Ultimate Reality, the Transcendent Truth, should always diligently try to manifest that truth in his speech. This quality of purity of speech by means of the vow of Truth, Satya, is of paramount importance. The importance of this great quality of truthfulness cannot be described by speech. Suffice it to say that if truthfulness is not there in the aspirant, his whole spiritual life is a wash-out. It is zero. There can be not an iota of real, substantial and lasting spiritual progress, unless one strives with all his might and all his heart and soul to stick absolutely to truth. In this there is no half-way house. A man is either truthful or he is untruthful. As long as he is not absolutely truthful, spiritual progress is only a hope or dream and it cannot be a reality to that aspirant. This is truth. Therefore, if people are serious, if aspirants are really earnest in their quest, if there is really a burning desire to somehow break the shackles of this mortal physical existence, this earthly life full of pain and sorrow, disease and ultimate death, if there is a longing to free oneself and enjoy eternal bliss, one must become an uncompromising votary of truth. Then only will Mother Saraswati be gracious and will bestow upon that aspirant Her Kripa; and he will get Knowledge of this Ultimate Truth. Let us every day unfailingly meditate upon this supreme virtue of virtues, this manifestation of Mother Saraswati in Her most glorious and most radiant form, this Truth, Satyam. A man must invoke the Mother as Truth; and he has established the splendour of the Atman in his heart. As long as that is not there, the light of the Atman cannot shine in that being. Therefore, let us always meditate upon Mother Saraswati in the form of truth. Truth is the greatest Yoga; it is the greatest Tapas and austerity in this iron age. A man who has got truth has got God. Let us always bear in mind this supreme importance of the Mother as truth. Let us meditate upon it. Let us reflect upon it. Let us always try by every possible means to gradually approach nearer and nearer to an absolute perfection of truth in our thoughts, in our words and in our deeds. May the Grace of Mother help us to achieve this very necessary, but very difficult task.

Speak Sweetly

Also language, the spoken word, is an all-powerful thing. It is a mighty force in this world of men. Language can be used to construct and to build as well as to destroy and to annihilate. We have seen how the great Mother as Saraswati is the essence of all constructivity. Therefore, let the seeker or spiritual aspirant ever be cautious as to how he uses this great power of speech. Let him take a vow never to hurt even the least of the Lord's creatures through any unconscious harsh word. Harsh speech, speech that pains, should be completely eliminated from the speech of the aspirant. One should speak sweetly. When it becomes difficult at any juncture to speak sweetly, it is better we remain silent. Of course, the next best, the third class, would be to immediately make up for any harsh word spoken, by expressing regret at once and trying to ask the forgiveness of him towards whom this harsh word is uttered. It is for those of the third class; but we should always aspire to belong to the first grade, Uttama Adhikari; our speech should always be sweet. Bear these three in mind: *Mita-Bhashana, Satya-Bhashana,* and *Madhura-Bhashana.*

Guard Your Tongue

Once again, as the constructive force in the world, Mother Saraswati should be used for helping others through our speech. Let not our speech be idle. If we speak, let us speak about the Lord, about the great ideal things, and also in order to console, to encourage, to inspire, to enlighten, to educate or to help in any way those with whom we have to speak with the power of Mother Saraswati. Idle-gossiping should be completely eliminated, in the life of spiritual Sadhana and the spiritual quest after Reality. Idle-gossiping is an insult to the Mother, as She is manifest in us as the mighty force of Vak or the spoken word.

Aspirants should never utter vulgar words. Habits die hard; and more so this holds good in reference to wrong habits. Right habits as sometimes are left behind more easily than the wrong ones because these wrong ones are firmly embedded in the lower self of the being; and whatever is there in the gross animal portion is very firmly entrenched through past repetition. Therefore, we come out of a world where speech is 75% indecent and 25% decent. To a vast majority of people, vulgar or indecent remarks are part and parcel of the ordinary conversation. They are not felt to be anything specially improper. But this same criterion should not be applied to the life of the spiritual aspirant. The aspirant must keep all objectionable words and terms out of his speech. His speech should be as clean as the flow of the pure waters of the Ganga.

These are the ways in which the aspirant can make Mother Saraswati manifest in him as the Suddha-Sattva. They are all spiritual qualities; they all lead to the increase of Sattva in him and they all indirectly contribute to his spiritual unfoldment.

Let us remember these various aspects of the

Divine Mother as-She is manifest in the inner path of
the Sadhaka, in Her Nivritti aspect. These are a few
that have been put before us. If we reflect over these
matters, we will find all the various ways in which
Mother tries to infill the personality of the seeker and
thus when we come to know what is opposed to the
qualities of Sattva, we shall be able to avoid those
things which are against the nature of Mother Saraswati, and we shall be able to diligently cultivate and
develop and increase those aspects of our inner life
and our inner nature in which She is predominantly
manifest, avoiding that which is impure and unspiritual
and growing more and more into the form of the pure
Sattvic nature. We shall be able to bring about ultimately the fullest unfoldment of the spiritual consciousness and we shall realise our Svarupa and attain
Svarupa-Jnana. We shall then be able to declare: "I
am neither mind nor body; Immortal Self I am."
*"Shuddhoham, Buddhoham, Niranjanoham, Samsara
Maya Parivarjitoham,"* *"Deho Naaham Jivo Naaham
Pratyagabhinna   Brahmaivaaham,"*   *"Satchidananda
Svarupoham."* These declarations are the spontaneous
utterances f the seeker who has adored Mother Saraswati with all his heart and obtained Her Grace and
has become illumined with the transcendent light of
the Supreme Atman whose First Emanation Mother
Saraswati is.

इडादेवहूर्मनुर्यज्ञनीर्बृहस्पतिरुक्थामदा निश ् सिषद्धिशे देवाः
सूक्तवाचः पृथिवि मातर्मा मा हि ूसीर्मधु मनिष्ये मधु जनिष्ये मधु

वक्ष्यामि मधु वदिष्यामि मधुमतीं देवेभ्यो वाचमुद्यास ̐ शुश्रूषेण्यां मनुष्येभ्यस्तं मा देवा अवन्तु शोभायै पितरोऽनुमदन्तु ।

ॐ

VIJAYADASAMI

THE GREAT GOAL AND ITS ATTAINMENT

तवामृतस्यन्दिनि पादपङ्कजे
निवेशितात्मा कथमन्यदिच्छति ।
स्थितेऽरविन्दे मकरन्दनिर्भरे
मधुव्रतो नेक्षुरसं हि वीक्षते ॥

TODAY is the glorious day of the celebration of
the Mother's Victory. It is a day of Vijaya, when all
the gods rejoice and all mankind is in an exuberance
of joy; for they have received the Supreme Assurance
that so long as they turn to the Mother in their ex-
tremity and distress, there will be no lack of support
and of strength. For, Mother is the champion of those
in distress and those who seek refuge at Her divine
feet. She is Strength Infinite, Maha-Shakti; and as
such we have but to turn to Her and no more will
weakness persist in us. The supreme victory over all
the forces of darkness, ignorance and nescience is
achieved and we shall be partakers together with the
Mother of joy of Vijaya. Vijaya-Dasami is a supreme

day of confidence, strength and courage for all seekers.

On this day all aspirants and those in quest of God have the greatest strength and courage for by the annihilation of all the forces that stand in the way of the fullest manifestation of divinity, Mother has thrown open the gateway as it were to the abode of Para Brahman. The worship of the Mother upon this supreme day is the worship of Maha-Maya in Her purest and absolute Vidya aspect. Till now, during the Navaratra, we worshipped the Mother in Her different aspects as She is manifest in this phenomenal world of human affairs. But when we come to Vijaya, we transcend the Mother in all Her external and Vidya-Avidya aspects and we gaze into Her face as the Pure Vidya-Maya, the Para-Shakti, to gaze at Whom is verily to gaze into the Infinite and the unfathomable depth of Para Brahman Himself.

For, we started at the very commencement of this worship by declaring that Mother is none else than the Para Brahman. The Supreme Being is Itself the Mother. Therefore, in Her Pure aspect as Vidya-Maya, She is Para Brahman Itself; and it is in Her radiant and all-glorious form of the Vidya, the radiance of Atma-Jnana, that we offer our salutations and adorations to the Mother upon this Supreme and blessed day of Vijaya Dasami.

On this day there no longer exists any element of the lower nature. There is no Asuric Sampat at all. There is no trace of demoniacal nature. All that is darkness has been completely annihilated. It has vanished. There reigns Mother and Mother alone in all Her supremacy. She is once again that mass of infinite consciousness. To invoke Her in this radiant, all vigorous aspect is to plunge ourselves in the supreme worship of the Transcendent ·Being. Thus, now, we start our worship and adoration of the Supreme Being, reaching which man has no more to go this round of painful birth and death. That is the abode of everlasting light from where there is no more return to sorrow. There is no more pain. Once for all we reach that supreme abode which is beyond all sorrow, all pain and all delusion. That is the supreme goal of the aspirant, the seeker, of all human beings, in fact, for this human birth has been given to us for that purpose of the highest attainment and for that purpose alone. All other pursuits are delusions and the one purpose of attaining the Supreme Being is the sole meaning, end and aim of this invaluable and precious human birth.

Guru: The Embodiment of Supreme Power

Upon this glorious day, let us take the opportunity of looking into one very great secret of the spiritual life. We have considered the Mother in Her threefold aspects of Durga, Lakshmi and Sarasvati, as She is manifest as different movements in this phenomenal existence, as different qualities in the aspirant and also as different forms of living and different phases of man's life and activities. But all this has been more or less in an impersonal way. She is also manifest in a special and an occult form; and this occult form of Her is in the nature of a divine personality. The manifestation of the Mother as our divine preceptor is a rare secret that is revealed to the heart of the spiritual seeker only through the Grace of the Lord, of Mother Saraswati. This secret of the direct personal manifestation of the Mother in Her supreme aspect of Vidya-Maya and Vidya-Shakti is the Guru to the disciple. She is the Sat-Guru to the seeker. To a spiritual seeker, that spiritual being whom he has accepted as his spiritual preceptor and the Guru is in the completest sense the visible personal manifestation and embodiment of the Supreme Divine Mother. Upon this conception of the Divine Mother rests the entire foundation of the seeker's spiritual life. Upon this rests the entire philosophy in Hindu culture. This is a unique conception the parallel to which cannot be found in any other culture upon the whole earth. This secret of seeing the Supreme Being as embodied and manifest in the visible personality of the Sat-Guru is at the very bottom of the success of the aspirant's spiritual quest. Thus, to every circle of spiritual seekers that particular personality whom they have surrendered themselves to and whom they have accepted in the core of their hearts as their spiritual guide, is the Supreme Embodiment of Para-Shakti, he is Brahma, he is Vishnu, he is Maheshvara, he is Shakti, and he is the Akshara Para Brahman Himself. This is a truth which no aspirant who is earnest in his quest for the Eternal can afford to lose sight of or miss or forget even for a single moment of his spiritual life. For him the human aspect of the Guru's personality should vanish; in its stead there should stand before him only the radiant embodiment of the Supreme Divine Power. This is an earnest reminder and a prayer to all aspirants and all seekers throughout the universe, be they of the East or of the West. This is a reminder also of the attitude which they should adopt towards their Sat-Guru, be they the followers of any spiritual personage whom they have accepted in the inmost core of their hearts as their spiritual Guru.

For, the degree and the measure by which we shall be fully aware of this special manifestation of the Mother in Her purest Vidya-Maya aspect in and through the living personality of the Guru, to that degree and in that measure will be the unfoldment of the divine knowledge in our consciousness; to that degree and measure will be the success of our spiritual realisations. Therefore it is that again and again the aspirant and the seeker who has surrendered himself at the feet of his Sat-Guru is reminded to worship the Guru-God; and the Slokas which all aspirants repeat every day embody this great secret and this highest truth:

Gurur Brahma Gurur Vishnu Gurur Devo Maheshvarah
Guruh Sakshat Param Brahma Tasmai Sri Gurave Namah.
Dhyanamulam Gurermurtih, Pujamulam Guroh-Padam
Mantramulam Gurorvakyam, Mokshamulam Guroh-Kripa.
Tvamhi Vishnur Virinchistvam Tvamcha Devo Mahesvarah
Tvameva Shakti-ruposi Nirgunastvam Sanatanah.

What is the real form of Guru? What should we feel he is?

Yasyantar Nadi Madhyam Na-hi Kara-charanam Nama
                                    Gotram Na Sutram

No Jatir Naiva Varno Na Bhavati Purusho No Napumsam
                                           Na Cha Stree
Nakaram No Vikaram Na-hi Jananamaranam Nasti
                                        Punyam Na Papam
No Tattvam Tattvamekam Sahajasamarasam Sat-Gurum
                                        Tam Namami.

In these glorious utterances we have a little of the great secret of this manifestation of Divine Vidya-Maya revealed to us.

The Quintessence of Great Scriptures

Upon this glorious day of Vijaya our worship of the Divine Mother in Her victorious Vidya-Maya aspect, this in reality constitutes the adoration of the Supreme Para-Brahman as manifest and embodied in and through the spiritual personality of the Sat-Guru. We have worshipped the Mother in various ways. Today we have specially tried to adore Her in the form of the written word, the lofty scriptures; the Vidyarambha with the reading of the Gita, the Brahma Sutras, the Bhagavata, the Ramayana, etc. Therefore, it will not be out of place to just mention in a few words what this approach to the Mother as the written word, as the scripture, She actually means to us. As I have tried to explain, Svadhyaya means a very special process to the aspirant. But it is also a practical way of life. The Svadhyaya is meant to mould our aspirations, our aims and ideals and our day-to-day living and actions also. Therefore, these scriptures— Gita, Brahma-Sutras, Bhagavata, Ramayana and the Mahabharata—contain a number of valuable lessons to us upon the spiritual path.

In a word, what is the great call of the Mother through the Bhagavad Gita? In the Bhagavad Gita, Mother has one supreme admonition and call, Tyaga. Gita means Tyaga; it is the scripture of the secret of renunciation. It says the one method of realising the Supreme is to renounce all that belongs to the phenomenal world—renounce your Kartritva-Ab-himana, egoism, attachment—to feel the whole universe is the Virat-Svarupa and that all your actions are worship of the Virat. Anasakti and Tyaga are the supreme admonitions given in the Gita.

In the Bhagavata we have the positive side. Renounce this phenomenal world; detach the mind from everything that belongs to this perishable world and have supreme love for the Lord. The one word which sums up the entire message of the Bhagavata is Love: love for the Lord. It is the radiant essence of pure Prem. It is Rati for the Lord. Gita teaches complete detachment; Bhagavata says: attach thyself to and whole-heartedly give thyself in complete oneness of love at the feet of Bhagavan.

The Mahabharata sums up the one ideal of sticking to Dharma. The Message of the Mahabharata is: even if life is to be sacrificed, do not deviate from the code of Dharma. Stick to Dharma even then. By Dharma one will be able to purify one's heart and life.

In the Ramayana the practical ways in which Dharma manifests itself in all the spheres of man's life are given. For, the Ramayana is a scripture which places before us concrete and practical living models of the ideal man of Dharma. It is a scripture which puts before us the moulds of the ideal husband, the ideal son, the ideal brother, the ideal wife, the ideal servant, the ideal seeker and the ideal king. The ideals of all these aspects of man's life in their detailed aspects are given in the form of concrete models in the various divine personalities of the Ramayana. If a man wishes to cultivate Love of the Lord and to live a life of Dharma, how then is he to conduct himself in his various aspects? For this the Ramayana gives the pattern upon which he may mould himself so that he may live a life of Supreme Dharma.

In the Brahma Sutras we are given the ultimate reason for all these things. It shows the supreme goal for which man has come. It says: the one purpose of this life is to reach the imperishable, that which is eternal bliss and to this end all these things are the means. Through the means you reach that Supreme Abode, reaching which there is no more return into the world of pain and death; for, the ultimate conclusion of the Brahma Sutras is that once having reached the Para Brahman through Dharma, Tyaga, Bhakti, *Na Punaravartate* the Jiva returns no more. He is once for all established in the transcendent, infinite consciousness, immortal existence, the eternal bliss, and perennial peace.

This is the goal. *Yadgatva Na Nivartante Tad Dhama Paramam Mama* says the Lord in the Gita. Having reached that Abode, man does not return to this world.

It is of the nature of Supreme plenitude. *Yo Vai*

Bhuma Tat Sukham. That Bhuma is the goal of man in this world.

Knowing which nothing else remains to be known. *Yasmin Jnate Sarvamidam Vijnatam Bhavati.*

Obtaining which there is no greater thing to be obtained. *Yam Labdhva Chaparam Labham Manyate Nadhikam Tatah.*

That is the glory, the supreme splendour of the transcendental state which we are all here to stirve for, to attain and to enjoy eternally. Thus, they have given us the goal and the ideal. The goal is Self-realisation. The means are the Tyaga of the Gita, the Bhakti of the Bhagavata, the Dharma of the Bharata, and the ideal life of the Ramayana.

We have gone through these supreme scriptures, to bring to our minds in its most vivid and intense form the aim and goal of human life, the means of its attainment and the practical pattern of the spiritual aspirant's life if he should attain the end through these means.

Prayer

Upon this day of the Vijayadasami which culminates the nine-days worship of the Supreme Divine Mother, let us all pray to Her that She may illumine our hearts as Buddhi, as Smriti. Let us all pray to Her that as Smriti She may ever keep alive these great truths in our hearts so that we may base our entire lives, mould our entire lives and conduct our entire lives upon a vivid consciousness of these truths. For mysterious is Her power as *Bhranti* and *Maya* that even though we know these truths we hear of them

again and again, and we try to remember them, yet
somehow in the twinkling of an eye, She makes us forget them; She makes us be only aware of these external objects of the sensual world. We forget these great
truths the moment Her veil is thrown over our consciousness. We become conscious only of things to in-
dulge in and things that give us momentary pleasure
and bind us to this external world of names and forms.
Therefore, we must pray again and again: "Mother,
manifest to us as the Vidya-Maya. May my consciousness be illuminated by Thy Vidya-aspect." As we have
seen just now, while reading the Devi Sukta, She is
everything—*Nidra, Kshudha, Chaya, Trishna, Bhranti,*
etc.,—at the same time She is Buddhi, Daya, Matha.
We should, therefore, fold our hands, bow at Her feet
and pray: "Ha, Mother! Manifest Thyself to me in Thy
illuminating aspect and save me from the aspect of
Thy Avidya-Maya." She will be propitiated; She will be
pleased; and She will open Her radiant eyes upon us;
She will smile upon us. Then all our delusion, all our
sorrow, all darkness will come to an end; and we shall
see Her as the Satchidananda Para Brahman.

These ten days we have tried to touch an infinitesimal fringe of the garment of the Mother. We
have tried to see if we may understand a little atom
of the Nature of the Mother. We may go on speaking
for hours and hours through all eternity, yet we shall
not be able to gain even a fraction of an idea of the
unknowable nature of the Mother. All scriptures, all
sages from eternity, have failed to express Her in Her
entirety. Therefore, it will be presumptuous for us to

think that through a few words, we have understood even a little fringe of the garment which the Mother has thrown over Herself and through which She hides Herself. What we have known is unto the grain of mustard; what remains unknown of the Mother is like the vast shores of the oceans. But, it is the love of the child that would make it approach the Mother and try to grasp Her hand and to know Her. Therefore, these ten days our attempt at trying to speak about the Mother has not been in the form of an endeavour to know Her—if She reveals Herself, then only can we hope to know—it is an attempt at a little flower-offering, a little worship at the feet of Divine Mother. Worship has been carried on during these nine days in is various ways. There has been music, songs, dance, decoration, Puja; and as one part of the worship, we have offered our adorations in the form of Her own aspect as Vak, which She Herself has given to us. We have tried to adore Her with words. And, upon this supreme day of Vijayadasami, we conclude this worship through words by offering at Her divine feet and praying to Her: "Mother, accept even this. Thou art love. Thou art compassion. Thou art illumination. Thou art release. Why to say all this? Suffice it to say: Mother, Thou art Mother. Therefore, as Mother, accept this humble offering of love at Thy Feet and may we all be blessed by Your Grace. Smile upon us, Mother; banish the darkness of Thy Avidya-Maya. Confer upon us all seekers at the Lotus Feet of this Divine Personality, our Gurudev, the radiance and illumination of Atma Jnana and the bliss of Satchidananda".